NO FEAR GARDENING

No Fear Gardening

How To Think Like a Gardener

CHARLIE HART

CONSTABLE

CONSTABLE

First published in Great Britain in 2020 by Constable

1 3 5 7 9 10 8 6 4 2

Copyright © Charlie Hart, 2020

The moral right of the author has been asserted.

A CIP catalogue record for this book
is available from the British Library.

ISBN: 978-1-47213-241-3 (hardback)

Typeset in Sabon by Hewer Text UK Ltd, Edinburgh
Printed and bound in Great Britain by Clays Ltd, Elcograf S.p.A.

Papers used by Constable are from well-managed
forests and other responsible sources.

MIX
Paper from
responsible sources
FSC® C104740

Constable
An imprint of
Little, Brown Book Group
Carmelite House
50 Victoria Embankment
London EC4Y 0DZ

An Hachette UK Company
www.hachette.co.uk

www.littlebrown.co.uk

For Isaac,
brave and sensible

Contents

Part III
Thinking like a gardener

Part IV
We must have vegetables

Part VII
Building projects & kit

Introduction

I was frightened of my garden. Terrified of getting something wrong or accidentally bringing death to a sap-filled friend. But it dawned on me that fear of error is a madness all of its own. If left unchecked it can become a terminal barrier to progress. At some point all the joy that I could see left unwrapped outside in my garden seemed to outweigh the little ball of fear that was keeping me from it. In that moment I picked up my secateurs and thought what the heck. At the time outside was a little garden in London, but it doesn't matter whether your garden stretches over acres or runs to a few window boxes. Fear must not be allowed to keep you from it.

Sometimes a ball of fear can be so big that the children's rhyme sums it up most accurately: 'We can't go over it, we can't go under it. Oh no! We've got to go through it'. To move through fear two things are desirable. The first is to make an unshakeable decision that you will jump. The second is to grab as much information as possible. This book is not an exhaustive record from the pen of an aged gardener, it is not even an expert's guide, but I hope it will leave you motivated to jump and ensure that you land, if not well, at least well enough to have justified the jump in the first place.

At over five acres, my current garden, Skymeadow in Essex, is by normal standards quite large. I have a mass of hedge to cut by hand, I have acres of grass to mow, I have all the new trees I have planted to manage, I have the flowerbeds to weed and plant and prune, I have the vegetable patch to tend and none of this includes 'new projects' that are undertaken each winter. I have no help. Sometimes I think of all this and a well of fear starts to bubble up inside. I am sure many people feel their to-do lists seem to trail off over the horizon of life.

But jobs that aren't being undertaken in the present belong to the future. And I must accept that either I will get round to them or I won't, and if I don't, I will deal with that fact then. In this way my garden forces me to live in the present, to hang up the heavy past and do away with the anxious future and instead to stand baggage free in the now. Otherwise every walk around the garden would amount to no more than a worrying list of jobs. Living in the present in this way is also what I mean by 'No Fear Gardening', or for that matter 'No Fear Life'.

I hope this book will be easy to dip into and out of as mood or opportunity dictate, but I also hope that if you are just getting into gardening you might enjoy reading it cover to cover, and that if you do you will feel you have been on a jolly green-fingered adventure.

I have tried to curate information on your behalf. You may wish to curate further. If I list five or so roses you may only find a home for one, but you didn't have to start with a hundred. Similarly, if I had given you all my thoughts on every type of evergreen hedge, this would very quickly have become a book on evergreen hedges. Instead I hope I have given you enough on evergreen hedges for you to get going and perhaps do some additional research yourself.

When it comes to plant names (and most have a great number) I have tried to use the one that it is best known by. Sometimes this *is* the Latin name and other times it isn't. For example, *Gypsophila* is probably better known by its Latin name than by its common name 'Baby's Breath' (though the common name is of course better). On the other hand *Hyacinthoides non-scripta* is likely better known in general conversation as a bluebell. I may sometimes have got these judgments wrong, or they may be peculiar to me and other gardeners would disagree, but my intention has been to try to use the name most commonly used. Occasionally, when disambiguating two plants with similar names I have provided the Latin in addition to the common name to better distinguish the two.

Before we start, I want to share one of the world's great secrets with you. Gardening is easy. Plants generally grow. Really, they do. If you don't believe me, stuff a couple in the ground and watch.

Part I

Getting underway

– *Gardening* –

What is a garden to you? You might think of a walled garden, or of the soft hazy pleasure of a rambling cottage garden but gardeners are just people who look after plants. A friend has a flat with no outdoor space in a large city. It does have a room with a large glazed roof and long windows at one end. In this room palm trees push up towards the ceiling, squadrons of succulents teeter about and there are a number of productive lemon trees. The whole picture is full and exotic and intense. My friend is a gardener every bit as much as any of us are.

I know from personal experience that I poured just as much passion, thought and attention into my little London garden (perhaps twelve feet by twelve feet) as I do into my current garden which is by comparison huge. If my garden amounted to no more than a carefully contrived collection of pots abutting a wall the same would be true. In fact, gardens comprised exclusively of pots can be overwhelmingly beautiful and demanding of a huge amount of skill. However large or small your garden is, and whatever sort of a person you are, the miracle of a garden is that it will multiply and repay the personal investment you make in it.

It is certainly the case that some are born with green fingers, some achieve them and some have them thrust upon them. Have you inherited a large garden? Have you acquired a small one simply because it came with the house you wanted? Are you interested in eating and desirous to make your urban terrace into a productive plot? Have you decided that you simply will not accept a world without plants and installed window boxes along the sunniest aspect of your terraced house? It matters not. If you tend plants you are a gardener. You will be paid in kind, with joy, peace, levity and the sure knowledge that you are helping our insect friends, capturing carbon, increasing the amount of oxygen in our atmosphere and quite possibly providing a square meal or two to boot.

When we bought our current garden I distinctly remember feeling immediately overwhelmed by the huge physical task of controlling (let alone improving) its over five acres of ground; ground that seemed constantly to be threatening to tip over into uncontrollable wilderness. My gardening career is at some level no more than the story of how I came to terms with that initial dread, of how this garden essentially forced me to adopt a no fear approach to it. Of all the complex matters that lay before me when we arrived six years ago, the question of how I was to cut the grass caused by far the most alarm. Specifically I had to work out what I would do, in amongst a sea of young children and work commitments, over five acres of grass on the one hand and the very real possibility I wouldn't have the time to cut it on the other. This developed into something of an obsessive worry.

Today, the central axis of our garden is an avenue of cherry trees beyond which the land falls dramatically into the valley so that the avenue seems to flow into the sky. On misty days the whole meadow seems to float as if moated by cloud, which of course accounts for how the garden came by its name: Skymeadow. Like much of East Anglia this place has a special relationship with the sky. But before the garden in any proper sense could happen, and before the sky could in any proper sense be enjoyed (by me anyway) I had to make some sort of accommodation with the grass.

– *Grass* –

M y initial solution to the problem of too much grass and not enough time to cut it was pigheaded. I tried to cut it all anyway. I threw myself at the problem not wisely but too well. I hoped that if only I tried harder it might all be okay. Actually, a cooler more strategic approach was required, but it took me a year or so before I realised that. My approach to grass is now radically altered, but I think it is worth unpacking why I went so wrong in the first place.

I had subconsciously been influenced by the doctrine of the pristine lawn. This is the general idea that lawns should be grass monocultures kept to a uniform height. For this to work properly they need to be stabbed, swept with sand, scratched, and worse, dowsed with poison. I didn't do any of that of course, but I thought that at the very least I should cut the thing. Today I recognise that the doctrine of the pristine lawn is not only supremely boring but it also robs a garden of variety, structure and wildlife.

These days there is no such thing as a regular weekend cut in my garden. Only the rose garden, the avenue and a patch by the house get even a vaguely regular cut. Any grass I can leave until the end of the season, I do. Where possible I mow paths through a grassy patch rather than topping it completely. This pays huge dividends aesthetically (because of the greater sense of height, variance and texture within the garden) but if you like butterflies to flutter by, bees to buzz and dragonflies to dazzle it is essential.

The orchid lawn in the rose garden gets two cuts a year, one at the end of the season and one in the early spring because this gives the orchid foliage a bit of a chance. Some parts of the meadow are left for a few years at a time so there is always some tussocky grass available for insects.

I don't understand what people have against moss. The Japanese often grow it in preference to grass and it usefully keeps its colour even in a drought; it is very welcome here. A pristine lawn seems to me the ultimate symbol of man's desire to control everything when all the fun is in letting it go a bit. When you do cut the grass raise the mowing deck to three inches plus and you will be rewarded with a carpet of herbs and flowers and whilst this massively favours insects it is far more interesting for us to look at too.

Whatever else, don't go cutting grass because you are frightened of it growing – like I did. Here is the truth: if you didn't cut your lawn for an entire season (never mind a missed weekend) it wouldn't actually matter, you could top it the following spring and no one would be the wiser. If you left it for two whole seasons it still wouldn't strictly speaking matter, but it might start to become a little tussocky. After three seasons a few tree saplings would start to establish and by four or five seasons the job of returning it to grass might be harder but by no means impossible. Missing a weekend is irrelevant. I suggest you leave perfect lawns to the Oxbridge colleges and now get on and enjoy your garden.

– *Plant nurseries* –

The first phase of my gardening life was dictated largely by the quality of my local plant nursery in London. Coincidentally I have found that in most parts of the UK there will be at least one smaller, family run or enthusiast led offering close by too, so it is worth googling who sells plants in your area at the outset.

There is a danger in getting overexcited on your first visit to a nursery. This is easily done because most nurseries are clever about arranging things in a way that is almost irresistible. However, plants are entirely seasonal commodities and if you blow a year's worth of your budget in the spring you will have a drab garden in the summer, autumn and winter. It really is best, crudely speaking, to divide your budget in four and visit in each of the seasons, coming away with a few trophies for each.

As a nation we don't much like talking about money. But the whole question of budget will likely have some bearing on your gardening life. These days we are awash with excellent high-quality plant nurseries in this country. Money no object you could broadly speaking wave your wand and create any garden you wished. The annual spectacle of the Chelsea Flower Show is evidence of that. But back in the real world there are a few basic pointers that I wish someone had shared with me when I started out.

The first (obvious in retrospect) is that it is always cheaper to grow a plant from seed or cutting than to buy it mature in a nursery. In our world, patience is generally a substitute for expenditure when you consider that many cuttings can be taken from a friend's garden and many plants can be multiplied from within your own.

Secondly, if a lack of patience can be expensive, impetuous purchases can be outright wasteful. If you simply can't resist a plant but you are unsure where you will put it when you get home exercise extreme caution. There is a significant danger you will end up planting it somewhere it doesn't want to be. Whilst this is not always fatal (many plants can be readily moved) I found to my cost that expensive Daphnes generally can't.

I love nurseries. I love the way they smell of nature, soil and plants. Frankly I like the fact that they often stock locally produced food and I don't even mind the assortment of tat (little slate signs that say 'garden this way' or 'love is the best'). I draw the line at gnomes (I dislike most anthropomorphic statues intended for gardens) but nurseries certainly provide their own sort of retail therapy. It is worth walking round them and looking at things even if you buy no more than a cup of coffee; I have learnt plenty doing just that. Nurseries at their best are incubators not just for young plants but for young gardeners too.

Because plants are so seasonal nurseries are a great place to identify plants you like. As you walk round the nursery you see this green bushy thing that seems to be everywhere at the moment and you turn the label round: 'eu ... phorb ... ia', bingo. In that moment you have become a gardener. Besides you probably know more about plants than you think you do and things will come back to you as you walk round – 'that is a foxglove, surely' you will say to yourself and as you turn the label sure enough it is; then you remember the foxgloves that used to grow in your grannie's garden and the whole matter of foxgloves falls back into place in your mind!

As you gain confidence you might start performing some basic checks on plants before you buy them. You might for example tap them out of their pots to check their roots. These should reach strongly to the extremities of the pot but not twirl round and round within it, otherwise the plant is pot bound. A pot bound plant will likely remain so even when you plant it into the soil. But you will also study the labels with far less anxious rigour before making purchases. Confidence just mounts without any single reason to justify its presence.

– Annuals, perennials etc –

For quite a while I seemed to find myself confused between begonias and bergenias (the latter known more commonly as Elephant's Ears). Their names sound similar and they both have attractive leaves but here the similarities stop and greater gardeners than I will at this point be laughing into their breakfast cereal. Still, the most important service an author can render is honesty and so I confess this fault with happy if rosy cheeks. As it happens begonias and bergenias are completely different plants from completely different plant families. Both come from far-flung parts of the world and both respond differently to our climate. But they do provide quite a good launch pad for a discussion about what the words annual and perennial actually mean.

Begonias come from the subtropics and, understandably therefore, shy at a British winter. Frost kills them. In the UK they can therefore only ever be grown outside as annuals (i.e. expected to survive for a single season). However, in their home climes they grow happily as perennials (i.e. they can be expected to survive for several seasons). Bergenias by contrast come from the Himalayas and so they think nothing of a dollop of snow. As such, they can be grown in this country as perennials. This distinction is made very stark when you stand in your own garden on Christmas Day and see the skeletal remains of a begonia dead in a pot on the table whilst a clump of bergenia glows bright in the border.

However, both begonias and bergenias are fundamentally perennial plants, they just respond differently to our climate. Nevertheless, some plants are true annuals. That is to say that whatever climate they happen to be growing in they will germinate, flower, set seed and then importantly die during the course of a single growing season. Sunflowers, poppies and love-in-a-mist are examples. Sometimes they die rather beautifully (think of the lovely seed heads left by love-in-a-mist) and sometimes less gracefully (like a great flopping sunflower that trips you up) but either way their strategy is to leave their children in the ground at their feet as their final act.

On which topic, plants that are good at coming back each year from seed are called 'self-seeders' and they are among my favourites. Different plants will come back more or less strongly in different gardens depending on how suitable that particular garden is for them. In my case both poppies and love-in-a-mist come back with great ease, as they will in most gardens. Sunflowers and marigolds will self-seed, but not so strongly. If I want to save sunflower seed I must gather them and put them in an envelope on my desk promptly because otherwise the birds will eat every last one.

Perennials by contrast are plants that live determinedly through many years. Each individual plant will survive winter and continue to grow the following season. Roses are perennials. Trees are the ultimate perennials. But just because each individual will live for many years this doesn't mean they don't flower and set seed too. All plants, trees included, flower and set seed. Perennials simply expect to raise a brood each year and survive the process!

Herbaceous perennials are just like normal perennials except that all their foliage above ground dies back over winter. However, the individual plant remains and reminds you of its presence when it breaks through the soil in the spring. A delphinium is a popular herbaceous perennial and so is an aquilegia, also commonly called a columbine. Some plants will also creep sideways under the soil. Mint is so good at doing this it will become an absolute weed if allowed to, but all plants with this habit will form expanding clumps and quite often the clumps can develop dead central sections, so gardeners tend to lift them periodically to split their roots out and replant the segments. This is called division.

Biennials are perhaps best thought of as stuttering perennials. Each individual plant may come back strong the following year but they may not, and with each year that passes the chance of their return becomes more haphazard. Wallflowers, foxgloves and forget-me-nots are all popular biennials. Gardeners start them the summer before they want to use them. Of course this requires forward planning (not one of my strongest suits) so if you forget you can generally start them in the spring and they may flower the same year or you may have to be patient and wait for them to flower the following year.

Technically a bedding plant might be an annual, biennial or even perennial. Either way gardeners typically buy bedding plants in large numbers in trays (petunias, pansies, begonias etc) and they are often used for a single season and then composted. This has always seemed somewhat wasteful to me so I am not the greatest fan. Having said that, bedding plants tend to sport the most garish and fun colours (think municipal planting scheme). Occasionally I am tempted at the nursery or supermarket to buy a few trays for my pots.

Whenever you buy bedding plants it is worth bearing a few things in mind. The chances are the bedding plants won't have been grown in the same conditions as are offered by your garden. Putting a plant in the ground is a shock to it, so is moving it to a new set of environmental conditions. Generally speaking bedding plants will thank you for separating these two shocks out. A few days spent in a sheltered spot in your garden in their trays prior to planting will help do this. That way they can adapt to the new environmental conditions before they have to adapt to being planted. Bedding plants being purchased from reputable suppliers will have also been watered regularly (to keep them smiling at punters) so they will resent a sudden cessation in that regard too. Finally, they aren't too keen on being crushed below a bag of shopping or being forgotten about for days in a hot car boot. You have been warned.

– *Acid or alkali* –

At the end of the introduction I said to you that gardening was easy and generally all you had to do was stuff plants in the ground and watch them grow. There is a huge amount of truth to this but one thing you can't readily change is your soil's pH. Your soil might be alkali or it might be acidic, but for ordinary purposes it is as well to know that there are a handful of popular plants (rhodies, azaleas, heathers and blueberries for example) that are truly acid-loving and simply won't thrive in alkali soil.

Strangely these are often the plants that people give me as presents. The answer, other than thanking the donor kindly, is of course to grow them in containers, where you can ensure they are planted into acidic soil. Use ericaceous compost bought from the nursery and mix it with some horticultural grit. It is worth saying that whilst acid-loving plants need acid soil, other plants generally don't mind it so compost leftovers can be used for other jobs too; though this might make pink hydrangeas blue!

Many friends excitedly dig these acid-loving plants into their alkali borders and I come back a year later to see a pathetic little dead frame. Don't bother. Why the gardening industry presents them as the present of choice, when you could just as well give a rose or clematis that would have a far higher chance of survival in most people's gardens, I don't know. Actually, maybe the answer is obvious.

If you have to have rhododendrons you could dig a giant pit and fill it with ericaceous compost but this would be very expensive and even then, without regular topping up, would probably still be pointless. My father-in-law had an old disused swimming pool in his garden and he had the idea of filling this with acidic soil – which might have worked because the structure would stop the soil leaching, whilst the cracks in the old concrete frame would facilitate drainage. But if you don't happen to have an old swimming pool with cracks in all the right places my advice would be to grow things that like the soil you can give them; trying to cheat nature usually ends in embarrassment.

If you have no idea whether your soil is acidic or alkali you can either buy a kit from the local garden centre or, I propose more cost effectively, simply have a look at what plants grow in close proximity to your garden. If you are awash with rhodies you are likely on acid soil, if your hedges are full of wild clematis, known to country folk as Old Man's Beard on account of its wispish excretions of facial hair, you are likely on alkali soil.

– *Types of soil* –

There are basically four types of soil: clay, sand, chalk and loam. You know if you garden on clay because if you gardened on sand you wouldn't be able to pick a handful of soil up and fashion it into the shape of a sausage – it wouldn't have the sticking capacity. If you can hold the sausage horizontally and it either doesn't lose its shape, or does so very slowly, you know you are on pretty claggy clay. Clay sticks because its particles are very small, sand doesn't because its particles are very large; all soil sits somewhere on that spectrum. If you garden on clay, don't panic, in some ways it is the best possible starting position, but you will have to leaven your clay by adding lots of organic matter. Adding organic matter as a mulch can be done whenever it isn't dry because although a mulch will hold water in the soil it will also keep it out. A slathering in the autumn and then again in the spring is a good starting point. Worms will work the mulch into your soil and over time it will become what gardeners call 'friable', which means easily workable.

Clay isn't easily workable; it sticks to the spade as you dig and can pan if walked over or compressed. Panning is a particular danger in a new build house whose garden has been traversed during winter by heavy machinery. When clay pans it makes a hard surface largely impermeable to water, essentially creating a little pond, and these little ponds can lie under the surface of a recently added top soil and either drown plants' roots or block them from making progress. In very extreme circumstances these areas need to be broken up and have organic matter dug into them. However, most of the time, adding significant amounts of organic matter as a mulch will, over time, leaven a clay soil. Some patience is required, but the rewards more than pay for the time spent waiting.

Unlike clay, sand has the advantage of letting water through, but it contains barely any nutrients. If you garden on sand you will have to enrich your soil, but interestingly, the method for doing this is the same as leavening clay: add organic matter. Whether you start on clay or sand you want to end up with loam. Loam has the nutrient quality of clay but the free draining properties of sand. Whatever soil you start with the path to loam is always the same: add lots of organic matter. When it comes to what organic matter to add, muck, homemade compost, bought in compost, mushroom compost (which is perhaps a little alkali) it doesn't generally matter, just add it.

Clay or sand can contain chalk and chalk will make the soil alkali. Most of England is on a large bed of chalk which runs from the north west to the south east becoming splendidly visible at the white cliffs. Chalk holds water very effectively (water moves through it very slowly) and more than that it filters the water as it goes which makes the huge bed of chalk England sits on into a handy giant aquifer. Water in the aquifer broadly speaking flows from the north west (where it initially falls as rain) to the south east (where it is extracted in its chalk-filtered state). The water we drink may have fallen on a stormy night somewhere in the midlands just as William crossed the Channel! This aquifer is one of England's great natural jewels but despite the fact that we all live on top of it few people seem to know it exists.

Particularly in the south east, there is a thick layer of clay above much of the chalk. The clay, being largely impermeable to water, acts as a barrier protecting the purity of the water in the aquifer below. As it happens, in my garden there is about a hundred and sixty feet of clay between me and the aquifer, but it would be a mistake to assume that my soil doesn't contain chalk. It contains lots of little pieces of chalk left over, presumably, from the original geological argument that bent and fashioned our valley.

Of course parts of England sit directly on chalk (think of the chalk streams in Hampshire that provide fishermen with such joy) and for that matter parts of Sussex sit directly (or more or less directly) on sand and gravel. Whatever you start with you want to end up with a rich friable loamy soil, and the journey towards such a state is half the joy of getting there.

– Growing from seed –

Whilst returning home from the nursery in triumph with a large mature plant delivers an immediate hit there will be a moment in every gardener's life when the desire to grow your own plants, from the moment of germination onwards, becomes simply irresistible. Whether you have a five-acre garden or a window box there is every benefit to starting your gardening life by doing what all gardeners love best, simply growing plants from seed.

The most intense period of seed sowing is during the spring and it is the time when I feel most like a true gardener. Setting the garden for the summer ahead is a big job and in addition to sowing seeds all the beds need weeding and mulching, the gaunt grey remains of last season's plants finally get cut back and stacked prior to composting. Any jobs half-finished over winter need to be speedily completed before things get properly underway. Every day my hands are in the soil and every evening my nails are caked with mud and I stagger as I rise from my armchair to go to bed. These are among the happiest days in the calendar.

When seed sowing is in full swing I am overcome with hope and I always have this sense of the sacramental. Perhaps there is something sacramental about the fact that you don't have to will a plant into being. Once the seed is set something new comes about and it does so entirely on its own, surely a physical and outward sign of an invisible grace! The mere fact of independent growth still astonishes me and no matter how many plants I grow the feeling never diminishes. Here is life itself refusing to be cowed by the grey rug of winter.

I tend to think of three great seed sowing opportunities in the year; the first is during late winter when you start seeds inside, the second is when the soil warms and you can sow seed directly outside and the third is after the last frost when it is time to think of what biennials you want to start for the following year. Accordingly I have suggested a few seeds for each window of opportunity. All are easy and will add real guts to your garden in one way or another. These plants will build a coronet around the perennials you have bought at the nursery and when you have grown each of these you will be familiar with most of the basic seed types and well positioned to move on to still greater things. Happy gardening!

– A few seeds to start inside –

During January and February the soil outside is unworkable (too wet and too cold to sow into) so no seeds (apart, perhaps, from the best adapted weeds) would readily germinate in it. The idea of starting seed inside during this period is to steal a march on the season. Some plants you start now, like tomatoes and squashes, need a long growing season but can't be planted out without protection until May, or perhaps even June in the north. Others, like salad leaves, can go out when the soil warms a little, usually in March.

Whilst all the seeds sown now should be started inside, inside need mean no more than a sunny windowsill. Many seeds once germinated are best positioned outside in a cold frame. A cold frame is small and cheap but does many of the jobs a greenhouse would do, just on a miniature scale. Some have wooden frames and glass panels but the more cost-effective ones have polycarbonate panels and metal frames. If you opt for the latter you will either have to peg them or weigh them down (or both) in order that they don't blow away. If a gale is forecast a few little patches of quality masking tape, enough just to stop the wind licking under the lid and pushing it up, will do the job.

I would be completely lost if I didn't have cold frames. I start all my seeds on trestle tables next to a sunny window in my study and try to get them outside into the cold frames as soon as possible in order to free up more space for sowing and germinating on the trestle table. A spring conveyor belt ensues.

Tomatoes and squashes are generally quite happy in my cold frames from March, but more tender plants like begonias or morning glory can be caught out even in a cold frame at this point. This risk can be greatly mitigated by filling up old milk cartons with water and placing them inside the cold frames. The water they contain retains the heat of the day and carries it into the colder parts of the night.

Seeds don't want an overly nutritious soil and they want decent soil drainage. Because you are starting the seeds in pots or trays you can choose the soil they will get. This is where the whole John Innes thing comes in which often confuses new gardeners. John Innes was a philanthropist who left money for an institute to be formed for the study of plants. The John Innes Centre near Norwich exists to this day. In the early part of the twentieth century two scientists at the centre, John Newell and William Lawrence, worked out what type of compost best suited seed sowing, potting on and final planting, in terms of both nutritional content and levels of drainage. Being kind folk they released this information (essentially compost recipes) to the public, free of charge. So when you see John Innes on the side of a bag of compost it isn't telling you who made the compost but what the compost is for.

In summary;

John Innes number 1 – compost with very little nutrition and sharp drainage so good for seeds and cuttings starting out in life.

John Innes number 2 – compost with a little more nutrition but still decent drainage so good for potting on.

John Innes number 3 – highly nutritious soil-based compost for trees.

23

In practice, unless I am potting up a tree, almost all the compost I use would conform to a John Innes number 2 recipe but with plenty of extra horticultural grit added. That seems to work for me.

Seeds generally want slightly elevated temperatures and a bit of moisture to get them over the hill of germination (some people find heated propagating mats helpful). In order to facilitate this I put a clear lid over my seed trays and sand-wich bags over my pots. But as soon as germination happens these covers must come off because after germination you want to dial down the heat to avoid mould and ensure that from the earliest possible moment seedlings begin to prepare for their life outdoors. Starting seeds inside is one thing but mollycoddling plants is a terrible idea because they will find life outside, when it eventually comes, more of a shock. It is a natural response for all new gardeners to try to give their prized little saplings a life of great comfort, but you will pay the price for it. This sort of mistake is rarely repeated the following season.

Sweet peas

The first sweet pea to arrive on these shores was Cupani, brought by the monk Francis Cupani from Italy in the seventeenth century. This is still, to my mind, the sweetest smelling. Some time in the nineteenth century Earl Spencer's head gardener noticed a sweet pea with a frillier flower than normal, and the 'Spencer' varieties were born. But whilst the Spencer varieties looked great, they didn't always smell as good as the older types. Modern breeders have attempted to combine the showy characteristics of Spencers with the scent of the old sweet peas. The true picture is far more compli-cated (there are grandifloras, dwarfs, heirloom varieties and more) but it is as well to be aware that there is sometimes a basic trade off when it comes to sweet peas; those with the most exuberance don't necessarily smell the best.

As a general rule it is worth growing sweet peas somewhere near the house because they need to be picked regularly otherwise they go to seed. Once they start setting seed they consider they have done the job they came to do and stop bothering to flower so I pick at least once a week, and often every five days.

Sweet peas are always the first seed of the year I sow, usually at the end of January. By the second week in February all of them will be outside in the cold frames which is where they remain until being planted out into their final positions some time in March. It is particularly important to move sweet peas somewhere cool as soon as they have germinated otherwise they will grow thin and leggy. You can grow sweet peas on the same patch of soil year in year out but if you do the soil needs refreshing every autumn. Mine gets a good dump of compost and muck, seven inches or more dug in.

You will read on many packets of sweet pea seeds that you should soak the seed overnight in warm water prior to sowing. I have never bothered and I don't believe I have suffered. I sow two seeds to a 3 inch pot. Some people put three in a pot. I use the backend of a biro to press little holes into the compost about half an inch deep. Into these go the sweet pea seeds. After watering I place a sandwich bag over the top and the minute the saplings appear off comes the sandwich bag. For an easier approach sow them directly where you want them to flower when the soil warms in March in little groups of three, but they will run the gauntlet of your slug population and you will have to be a little more patient for a flower.

The consensus of opinion is that it is best to pinch the top off sweet peas once they have reached a few inches of height. This encourages bushier plants that flower for longer. I pinch the top off every other in the hope my sweet pea stands will grow both bushy and tall.

Tomatoes

Sowing, growing and eating your first tomato is a milestone for any gardener; it has the heady scent of arrival within the conclave of the green fingered. It has long been thought that growing basil next to your tomatoes improves their flavour so I always do and my tomatoes always taste great. Whilst I fry tomatoes for breakfast, or with meat for dinner, and I sometimes bake them for the purposes of a pasta sauce I most commonly pop them in the salad bowl along with five or six handfuls of basil; so having the two growing close to each other makes scavenging for lunch easier.

I start my tomatoes on or around Valentine's Day in a tray filled with compost and horticultural grit. I place the seeds themselves on the surface and give them a light dusting of compost (really just a pinch) and a generous blast with my atomiser which is filled with lukewarm (not cold) water. The trays get covered with a see-through lid and put in the sunniest spot on the trestle table. Within a day of the seedlings cresting the compost the lids come off because they will start going rotten and mouldy quite quickly. Once the little seedlings have two true leaves they get pricked out into their own 3.5 inch pots (though you could use 3 inch ones). As with all seedlings only ever hold the leaf, never the stem, when pricking out.

I use the flat end of my trusty biro to make a planting hole in the pot and quite often the pointy end to lever the seedlings out of the tray. As I lower the seedling into its own pot I make sure to bury it far deeper than it was in the tray, dropping the stem right into the pot so that only a sliver of it is visible above the compost. This gives the tomato the chance to make new and better roots from its stem and this method works when potting up plenty of seedlings. The same logic can be applied a second time when you eventually set the plants out in the garden.

It is relatively simple getting a tomato sapling to a healthy and happy state growing away in its own individual pot in your cold frame by, say, the middle of March. The main dilemma is that they can't be set out until after the last frost sometime in May. As a result at some point in April they start to look like they really would prefer life in a vegetable bed rather than life in a pot. My solution is to plant them out under a large bell cloche sometime towards the end of April. When I plant them out, I place lots of large flints around their base, partly to help anchor them and keep moisture in the soil and partly, as with milk cartons in the cold frames, to carry heat from the warmth of the day into the cooler parts of the night.

Tomatoes are hungry plants so when you do get round to planting them make sure they are planted into soil that has been lavishly enriched with compost and manure the previous autumn. I plant mine with almost three feet of spacing and give each plant a bamboo cane as a support.

If you want to follow my system choose cordon varieties that are suitable for outdoor growing. As the plant grows you will notice between the main trunk and the principal branches new branches emerge at 45 degrees. These can be pinched out to improve your harvest. The main stem (known as the growing point) can also be pinched out once it reaches an acceptable height. That said, I have grown cordons without

27

bothering and been left with terribly messy sprawling plants that still yielded a perfectly good harvest. Towards the end of the season it can be profitable to pinch away foliage that is shielding fruit from the sun and therefore stopping it from ripening. If you are left with some green tomatoes they can of course be used to make chutney and held against the forthcoming winter!

It is perfectly possible to grow a decent crop of tomatoes in a pot. If you wish to do this try to use the largest pot you can bear (tomatoes are quite hungry) and make sure they get lots of direct sunlight. If growing in a pot it is probably best to choose appropriate varieties (smaller bush types) so think about this when making your seed order. Otherwise, if you have just a little more space (for example a terrace), a very good crop can be grown in a tomato grow bag. These are like bags of compost that you lie on their side and plant directly into. Many vegetables can be grown perfectly well in grow bags and I have used them often for courgettes and sometimes afterwards for a second crop of salad. Cut neat little holes to plant into and remember to make a few holes in the bottom for drainage.

Don't get too weighed down with rules even when it comes to the racy and exotic tomato. Last year I found several good tomato plants that went on to fruit growing in the gravel against the north-east facing wall of our house. I hadn't planted them there and so I scratched my head in bewilderment. I remembered the previous summer our kitchen drain had blocked and created a sort of large puddle over the adjacent gravel. These seeds must have germinated from some washed off a chopping board! Seeds grow, really they do.

Squashes

I love squashes, marrows, cucumbers, courgettes and even gourds and all are cucurbits. Gourds are not edible but I grow them to decorate the dining room table at Christmas. I have recently discovered a French squash called Potimarron which has an excellent nutty flavour and can be chopped into cubes, smothered in olive oil, and baked with sprigs of rosemary or doused in smoked paprika. Minced meat or cheese (or both) can be added if appetite demands. However, the all-time favourite in this household remains Patty pan, or as my children call them 'flying saucers'. These roll in all summer and it is the simplest thing in the world to scoop the seeds out and stuff them before baking for a meal in one. I stuff mine with a special cheese and fresh basil paste I make for the purpose.

Cucurbits are a bit like tomatoes in that they benefit from a good long growing season in order to crop and fruit. I start them a few weeks after the tomatoes sometime in March, and they go into the cold frames sometime in April and then follow the tomatoes out into the garden – but again with a delay of a few weeks. All cucurbit seeds are large so they can be sown directly into pots. The most common cause of disappointment with cucurbits is that they don't germinate (usually because they have rotted). Minimise this risk by adding lots of horticultural grit to your compost mix and *always* push the seed into the mix pointy side down. Sowing into a 3 inch pot is the technical advice (a smaller pot makes rotting less likely) but I sow mine into 3.5 inch pots because I know they will be sitting in them for a while. Once sown, water and cover the pot with a sandwich bag. The minute you see a sapling, off comes the sandwich bag!

There is something of a trade off with respect to when you set squashes out. They like the cold even less than tomatoes, though on the other hand I want them to start setting their roots down at the earliest possible moment. I tend to take the plunge at some point in early May though, just like the tomatoes, to begin with they go out under bell cloches and they also get a mulch of flints to keep moisture in and to deliver some thermal effect at night. Holding some seed back to sow directly is one way of taking out an insurance policy!

Just to clear things up, summer squashes are harvested as they ripen in the summer and tend to grow on bushes. Their skin can often be eaten. Winter squashes are harvested in the autumn and tend to grow on vines. Their skin is hard to the point of being very difficult to cut into. Patty pan would fall into the former category and Potimarron the latter. If courgettes get a little large they can be good for stuffing and baking but generally you want to harvest them promptly.

Lettuce

Whilst growing lettuce can be a bit of a fiddle, I like eating it, particularly if it is slathered with a blue cheese dressing and even more so if a steak is involved. One of my favourite celebratory dinners involves cutting a large wedge out of an iceberg lettuce and placing a steak that I have just fried in garlic gingerly on top of it before covering the whole with a blue cheese dressing. Many years ago I learnt to my delight just how easy it is to cobble together a passable blue cheese sauce. Simply wet the bottom of a pan with full fat milk and crumble a block of blue cheese into it. Heat but don't boil and then pour!

It won't surprise you to learn therefore that I always grow some sort of crunchy iceberg type lettuce. However, I also like to grow lettuce with unusual textures and I always grow a red lettuce to spruce up the salad bowl. There are thousands of types of lettuce and as with most vegetables I grow a few favourites every year and trial a few new varieties too. Every now and then a new variety will knock an old favourite off its spot.

When you choose seeds don't be put off by the different classifications (crisphead, butterhead, romaine, iceberg etc): that just relates to the shape of the lettuce once it has grown not to how you grow it. Lettuce seeds are small and fiddly so as with tomatoes (and unlike sweet peas) they should be started in a seed tray. With lettuce seeds tamp the compost in the tray down with the back of your hand and make three lines across it with the end of the biro and run some seeds along the drills you have created. Leave a good inch and a half between each seed. Also, don't be tempted for symmetry to line the seeds up, rather have them alternating in each row so each plant will have the most space possible for its roots to grow. Water, place a lid on the tray and position in a sunny spot. Seedlings will appear within a week or so. Remember as soon as the seedlings crest the surface of the compost . . . off comes the lid.

Some people prick out the seedlings and grow them on in individual pots. I find it is best just to let them grow on in the seed tray and when they are quite large prick them directly out into the ground in the garden. The larger the plants are when you finally plant them out the more likely they will be to withstand attention from slugs and snails. Unless you are growing a small variety it is worth giving each lettuce as much as two hands (for the rest of this book, a hand means the distance from the tip of the thumb to the tip of the pinky when the hand is fully outstretched) distance from its neighbour. As with the tomato seedlings you can plant them deeper into the ground than they were growing in the tray so that the plant makes new and stronger roots from its buried stems.

The absolute secret to growing good lettuce is to keep it generously watered. If it gets too hot it is a disaster; the plant just stalls and stops tasting nice. This often happens in heat waves but there is nothing you can do about it so move on to something else and compost the lettuce. Whichever way you look at it, starting a couple of seed trays of lettuce by your kitchen sink is easy enough and within a month or so you will be able to repeat those hallowed words to your friends when they come to lunch: 'Yes, the lettuce is from the garden'.

Wild strawberries

In Rome in July there is a festival dedicated to the wild strawberry (also known as the woodland or alpine strawberry). The Italians are truly sensible people and the Romans, particularly, prioritise what is important in life. I have sat in Rome in July and eaten a bowl of wild strawberries, the midsummer heat catching and carrying the true strawberry scent with each mouthful. They serve them simply (a large bowl of the miniature strawberries with nothing other than a scoop of vanilla ice-cream) and this is wise, because if one did a Wimbledon on them it would obfuscate what is, to my mind, one of the most delicate and surreal flavours in the natural world.

Drowning our English strawberries in cream and sugar is not so silly because the strawberries themselves very often don't taste of much, other than water, which is why I grow wild strawberries. I grow them in the rose garden (where they make an excellent ground cover for the roses), they are in the vegetable patch, they are in the snaking sweet pea border and they have a whole bed dedicated to them next to the house. You need to grow them on scale if you are serious because they yield far more lightly than normal strawberries. But even if you only grew one plant and had one small bowl a year it would still be worth it.

Strawberry seeds are our first really small seed and I sprinkle a pinch of them across the surface of the compost in a seed tray and then tamp it down gently with the back of my hand. Water them and put a see-through lid over the top of the tray. Once the plants emerge they should be potted on but I have found it is useful to pot them on into something smaller than a 3 inch pot (something more like 1.5 inches) in order that they don't end up dampening off (failing in a soil that is holding too much moisture). Probably you should then pot them on again but I don't, I just give them a spell in the cold frame and plant them out when they look like a nice little plant. In good years I will introduce fifty or a hundred new plants to the garden here.

A variety called Mara des Bois is half wild and half cultivated and cosseted by French chefs. I grow cultivated (non-wild) strawberries too. They break down into early, mid and late season varieties. If you are starting a bed of cultivated strawberries it is generally advisable to choose some from each category to ensure continuity of supply. Wild strawberries on the other hand are ever bearing, which means they fruit more lightly but throughout the season.

Cultivated strawberries want cutting back at the end of the season, to remove diseased foliage, and a good mulch in the spring for food. They send out runners readily and these create little plantlets. When they are big enough they can be detached from the parent plant and set in their own positions. This should be done periodically because many strawberry plants will hit their peak of production in the third year and then tire.

Most cultivated strawberries are bought in pots or trays and can be just popped into the ground. Some strawberries come as bare root crowns – these will arrive in the spring and you must soak them in water for at least an hour. Afterwards build a little volcano of soil and place the crown on the top of it before spreading the roots out like spider's legs and covering. You don't want to bury the crown itself too deeply under the soil otherwise it may rot.

– A few seeds to sow directly when the soil warms –

When you are sowing seeds directly into soil outside the perfect moment to start is dictated by the weather (which as we know can vary from year to year). You will have to use your instinct. Choosing when to sow something isn't about being punctual with the calendar, it is an attempt to give the seed what it wants. The time to sow seed directly outside is when the soil is dry enough to work and warm enough to germinate seed. The traditional way farmers used to test the warmth of the soil was to drop their drawers and sit on it. However, another less immodest way is to look and see if all the weed seeds are germinating; if so this is a reliable indicator that the soil is warming, but not necessarily yet where you want it to be.

Every year the right moment comes on a slightly different day but if you just take a calm moment and listen strongly to your instinct, even without gardening experience, I bet you will start calling it right each year. We are all descended from people who did this every year and their lives depended upon it. You have the software preinstalled. In this garden the day might come in March, or it might come in April; every year is different.

Whenever the day comes, there is something deliciously easy about sowing seed directly into the soil where it is to grow. Particularly because I have limited space indoors, I try to sow as much as I can directly.

My only real obstacle to sowing seed directly is our cats. Our cats are quite good at not damaging young plants and will generally choose bare soil to do their business (most obliging of them). The trouble is that soil containing newly sown seeds looks to a cat like perfectly bare soil. Trouble mounts when a giant Labrador then tries to retrieve the gift the cat has left (don't ask) and the whole bed is trampled! As a result I often set bamboo canes around an area of freshly sown seed and tie string to it at cat level. (Remember that the end of a bamboo cane, wherever you find it, can be dangerous and you certainly don't want to poke yourself in the eye whilst bending over a bed so be careful.) I also stick foot-long twigs randomly into the ground so the cat thinks something is going on. We manage, after a fashion.

Remember seeds don't want to float upon or within your garden's soil, they want proper seed to soil contact. Larger seeds can and should be gently pressed into the soil. I make sure the drills I prepare have lightly compacted bottoms. If you are pinching out really small seeds tamp the soil down afterwards with the back of your hand or boot and always make sure you water seeds in (without washing them away).

Poppies

There is nothing that engages the eye in such a moment of captivation, such a *coup de grâce* for an otherwise miserable soul, as the vision of a blowsy poppy, caught, perhaps, by a gentle breeze and illuminated by a bright optimistic early summer sun. Poppies have a sensuality, delicateness, vulnerability all of their own. But don't be fooled, their seeds can survive for decades underground only bursting forth when disturbed, which is why they litter building sites and why, of course, they littered the Somme.

The whole matter of poppies will be a good deal easier if I introduce you to the four types of poppy you are most likely to encounter. The poppy of the Somme was of course the field poppy (*Papaver rhoeas*). When plants have the name 'field' attached to them it really just stands for common, as with field maple. But the poppy that first stole my heart was the Californian poppy (*Eschscholzia californica*). The classic shade for this is a rich golden orange. The flowers open in the morning and follow the sun throughout the day. Touchingly, they tuck themselves up at night.

If my love affair with poppies started with the small and simple Californian type it quickly progressed to the opium poppy (*Papaver somniferum*). These are large creatures held high on glaucous silvery blue foliage. This is the ultimate blowsy summer poppy, and in the moment when one is before me my favourite possible plant. Opium poppies come in a large range of pastel colours but a deep red and soft purple are most common in my garden. Save the seeds from the ones you like most.

For completeness there is a fourth type of poppy I grow, an oriental poppy (*Papaver orientale*). These are herbaceous perennials and it is simplest to buy plants in pots (though they can be brought on from seed). Oriental poppies grow in a shrubby form and have curious names like Patty's Plum, Royal Wedding or Snow Goose.

The loveliest thing about starting annual poppies in your garden (and if you will only have one type, opium poppies) is that whilst you choose a spot for them in the first year, before long they start choosing their own spots. Their capacity to find and fill bare patches in a bed or border is unparalleled, which makes them rather good if you are running a garden on a budget.

My method for sowing these sorts of hardy annuals is to scatter them where I want them to grow. Rake the soil over and cast seed out in pinches before tamping down with the back of your hand and watering. The watering pushes the little seeds into the cracks of the soil and ensures contact, though use the correct size of rose on your watering can so you don't just wash them all into a gully. Nothing could be much easier than that.

The only downside to sowing any flowering annual in this way is that when it germinates it will do so alongside weeds. Actually poppy seedlings are easy to differentiate but if you are at all worried when you are sowing seeds an old gardener's trick is to pinch them out into lines that either zig zag or cross. That way when you are weeding you can leave the zig zags or crosses and hoick everything else out. You might worry this will result in a zig zag flower display. It never does.

Love-in-a-mist

If you are after the English cottage garden look love-in-a-mist, also commonly known as Nigella, is a must. As with forget-me-nots and poppies, love-in-a-mist is a great flower to use to fill sunny gaps between perennials. It has feathery geometric foliage which seems to coalesce into a green mist in the border (hence the name).

Start love-in-a-mist when the soil warms as you would with poppy seeds. Once the seedlings start into growth thin them out quite ruthlessly otherwise they grow poorly as a pack. You probably want a hand of distance between each plant. You can also start them in September for flowering the following year, as with a biennial.

Love-in-a-mist self-seeds very strongly and in addition to having little communities of it in the rose garden it has quite happily taken up residence in my sunnier patches of gravel. I let hollyhocks self-seed in gravel, along with poppies and lavender – it perks the whole thing up no end. I think love-in-a-mist should really be either white or blue but there are pink varieties on offer too.

Nasturtiums

Nasturtiums add value to your garden year in year out. Once started they will reappear every year and they work wonders running along a path or spilling out of the edge of a raised bed. I started out my gardening life particularly in love with the deep crimson varieties like Empress of India but I now rather like a variety called Crème Troika. They will keep flowering vigorously right up to the first few frosts and their leaves make a peppery addition to a salad.

Nasturtiums don't want an overly rich soil and if you give them one they will produce lots of foliage but fewer flowers. Not that this is a bad thing because their foliage is, to me at least, just as mesmerising as their flowers. As with Californian poppies, the little seedlings seem to track the sun across the sky like little green satellite dishes. Nasturtiums can get a little bolshie and crowd other things out so once you have a resident community a judicious thinning in the late spring or early summer, particularly from the centre of beds, might be wise.

Nasturtiums are big fat seeds that can be easily manhandled by little fingers which makes them a good choice if, as I do, you quite often find yourself gardening with toddlers. My method is to simply push the seeds half an inch into the soil in little groups of three where I want a clump, usually in April. I plant them in the garden and also in little pots scattered around garden tables.

Sunflowers

What sunflowers lack in refinery they make up for with drama and fun. Most people associate sunflowers with the giant Russian variety but actually there are quite a few more sensible sunflowers and some have lovely russet, amber or golden shades. I grow one with my daughter Florence each year and it comes to be known as Florence's sunflower. This year's was unusually bushy and evenly adorned with very many sensibly sized flower heads. It was every bit as subtle and interesting as any other flower you might wish to grow. I wish I could remember which variety it was.

Large sunflowers may need to be staked if they are not to flop all over the place. The bushier varieties will take care of themselves. Sometimes pinching out the first few flowers can create a bushier plant in the end. Other than their ease and the speed with which they repay the effort the great benefit of growing sunflowers is that they keep the birds going through autumn and winter like nothing else. Growing a sunflower is growing a bird table for the cost of a packet of seeds. So long as you get there before the birds, sunflowers also make very good candidates for collecting your own seed. If you choose seeds from the sunflowers that have performed the best, over time you will end up with super sunflowers genetically selected for the conditions of your garden.

You can start a sunflower inside earlier in the year if you wish but my method is to sow them directly where they are to grow in little groups of three, with the best being preserved and the others either moved or slung. Push the seeds into the soil half an inch and water. I find it better to start them later and sow them directly because they germinate and take off in one go and seem to do better than those started inside. May is a good month. As their name suggests they don't like cold and they do like sun.

– A *few seeds for the summer* –

There is of course no way of telling for sure when the last frost will be because it would require a level of prophetic aptitude rare even among gardeners. However, history is a good indicator and there are frost predictors online that will tell you the average time for the last frost in your area.

Think about the position of your garden. Everyone knows heat rises and cold falls but this is true in gardening terms too. If you garden at the bottom of a valley you might have a slightly later frost than a comparable location slightly further up the hill. Cold moves and flows like a river and surprisingly is kept in position by barriers. In other words, cold will roll down the hill unless it meets a wall which will hold it in place. It is funny to think of heat and cold in these aquatic terms but it is accurate to do so. In my garden (which is on a leaky hill) the last frost is assuredly behind us sometime in May and this marks the point at which the garden enters the full whirligig of summer.

Of course, one of the very great benefits to an urban garden is that cities provide very significant protection from frost and larger cities will often be a degree or more warmer than the countryside that surrounds them. This actually has the effect of extending the season. For example, the tulips in the garden at Buckingham Palace will come out weeks before they do here! If I gardened in a city now I would concentrate on using this effect to push the boundaries of what was possible and likely focus on relatively exotic plants: vines, peaches, grapes, figs and the like.

Nonetheless, once the last frost is behind you it is time to place out those tender squashes that you started in March and any other tender plants you might have on the go that haven't already gone out under cloches. But there are still seeds to be sown afresh, especially biennials. Organised gardeners will typically start biennials in June (or even May) either under glass or in a nursery bed and then transplant them into their final positions in September. The plants will then establish a little before the first frost, sleep through the winter and be ready to spring into action first thing the following year. Not being the most organised gardener I have in the past sown many where they are to flower towards the end of summer and got away with it. In any case I urge you not to discount this merry band of plants simply because they require a little forethought. They are the real joy of summer seed sowing.

Foxglove

For some reason, almost everyone knows what a foxglove looks like. Perhaps it is because our mothers told us not to eat them when we were young and the warning has somehow singed itself into the collective subconscious. Foxgloves are poisonous and have a chemical in them that will affect the heart (they were used to treat people with dropsy before medicine moved on, but it was a risky business because the line between medicine and mortuary was fine). I tend simply to use gloves when I handle them and have never returned to the house with a racing heart, at least not on account of this flower.

Foxgloves at their best are as beautiful and beguiling as any plant can be; they have an unhurried and proud demeanour and a sort of surety within an overall garden scheme that is grounding. I sometimes wish they grew a little taller, but there it is. We sometimes imagine them to be bigger than they are but I suspect this also has to do with our having met them first as children, when they were bigger in relation to us.

You can buy varieties that are different colours (white is a popular one, for example) but within a few generations this will be lost and they will revert to their natural colour, which is not a problem as far as I am concerned. Foxgloves are one of the plants that will self-seed fearlessly within most gardens so once introduced you will never have to say adieu. As a rule I have found they prefer partly shaded positions with moist soil. An east facing bed along our barn gets a little sun in the morning but never enough to challenge the bed or to burn off the moisture in the soil. Foxgloves love it. If you introduce foxgloves anywhere, they will generally find their own way to their favourite spots in your garden.

It is easiest to start foxgloves where they are to flower in June. The seeds are very small so pinch them out over the soil and then keep it moist. When seedlings appear thin them out so each individual plant has a decent amount of space (over a hand, anyway). The excess little plantlets can be moved with a trowel and used elsewhere if you wish. The following year the plants should flower in May. To prolong flowering cut the principal stem and subsidiary ones will appear from the base.

Wallflower

The first thing to note about wallflowers is that they smell heavenly, and theirs is among the first really exciting scents you sniff as spring rises around you. The fact that they flower early has also made them a traditional companion for tulips.

Despite the fact that you can buy them in a number of colours I have come to the conclusion that wallflowers really should be, as they traditionally were, a glowing golden or russet colour if they are to look and smell just right. Bowles's Mauve, which in any case can't be brought on from seed, is a pleasant blue (and it has its uses, including a long period of flowering) but it just feels to me like a different plant.

The question with wallflowers is always what to do with the space when they finish flowering. If they flank a path or roughly edge a bed this is less of an issue. Most people grow wallflowers as bedding plants and then bin them but I have noticed individuals flower on for several years. They will seed very easily and so wherever you put them to start with, if you don't cut them back or pull them out, they will etch out communities in strange places within your garden – they are as happy in a crack in a wall as anywhere else. Perhaps this is the best way to enjoy them.

I think it is easiest to start wallflowers outside in May or June where you want them to flower. If this is inconvenient they can be started elsewhere in a nursery bed and moved to their final flowering positions in September. They will break into flower the following March (though odd weather can bring them into flower earlier, even in the autumn). If you give them enough room they will grow quite large, a few feet up and out anyway.

Forget-me-not

If you grow roses cast forget-me-not seeds in amongst them. A carpet of forget-me-nots will give the rose bed a lift just when it needs it but will not do any damage to the roses, or to anything else for that matter. Over the years I have introduced lots of different forget-me-nots to this garden. Sometimes I have bought plants or dug a clump up from a friend's garden, but more often just scattered seed where they are to grow in late summer. Use the same method as for poppy seeds: pinch them out over freshly raked soil and tamp gently with hand or boot.

In addition to pale blue some come close to a wispish cloudy white colour and some a sort of sparkling violet that has an astonishing depth to it. There are pinky whites too. Some in this garden now have impossibly small flowers. I am certain that over the years, as bumblebees have visited clump after clump, we have strains that are all our own.

After forget-me-nots finish clear away the grey stalks (this can be done by just running your hand through them) so they don't cast too much shade on their babies the following spring. A single stem of forget-me-not in an egg cup on my desk at the end of winter is as good as a dozen roses in high summer, delicate sprays of the most sensual pale blue imaginable; it is a colour that could launch not just a thousand but ten thousand ships.

Hollyhock

In the summer we often go to Blakeney on the Norfolk coast for a little holiday. Walking down the High Street is a pleasure all of its own. Not simply because of the medieval scale, or the way in which the village seems dug into the Norfolk coast in the most cosy way imaginable, or because of the lovely and consistent use of un-knapped flint in all the buildings and garden walls but because of the huge array of hollyhocks that have self-seeded into every crack, slit, nook and cranny all the way down. Hollyhocks do tend particularly to like the east, I think it must be the fact that we get a little more sunshine and a little less rain.

Some grow monstrously tall (brandishing flowers at over ten feet) but there are always flowers at the perfect height for a toddler to stand and stare too. There are a very wide array of colours: almost whites, almost blacks, seemingly purples, pinks, apricots, crimsons and yellows. They flower progressively up their wands and they spill thick golden pollen that seems to crumble as it tumbles down the side of the crêpe-like petals. The bees love them.

Known alluringly once upon a time as St Joseph's Staff, hollyhocks have fallen out of fashion probably because they are quite prone to rust that mottles their leaves. This is a pity, because with or without a little rust here or there, they are plants that cause a huge amount of pleasure. I have them growing in my gravel but also towards the back of flowerbeds. I have favourite individuals too. One in the herb garden at the moment whilst not black is such a dark purple it seems to be luminous at a distance. It is absolutely worth keeping the seed from the ones you like. A little envelope with a nice inscription containing ten or so of the precious seeds isn't a bad present either.

The seed itself is attractive, and pressed flat like a botanic gold coin it seems to be an appropriate store for such a promising strand of double helix. Hollyhocks are excellent overwintering stations for ladybirds so I leave mine until the spring but if you were particularly worried about rust it would be worth cutting their stems down in the autumn to remove disease from the area where the plants are growing. When you save seed do so from plants that seem relatively clear. Hollyhocks flower late-ish in the season so they can refresh an otherwise slightly flat August garden. The single-flowering varieties are far better for bees than the double-flowering ones. I have purged this garden of double-flowering ones and will no longer buy them.

I have started hollyhocks very early in the season (February or March) inside in pots. I sow three seeds to a pot and then keep the best seedling for planting out properly by May. It would be less wasteful of seed to start them in trays and then pot on the resultant seedlings. I start them early in the hope that I might get flowers the same season (and I often do) but it would otherwise be perfectly sensible to sow them directly in the summer for flowering the following year.

– Plant families –

Now that we have engaged with the real messy business of growing plants from seed it might pay to double back to some theory. Because there are so many plants it has been necessary to break them down into families in order to make head or tail of them. This is a perfectly sensible step and the whole endeavour was kicked off by the Swedish botanist, Carl Linnaeus, in the middle of the eighteenth century. Sadly, as science has discovered more about plants, specifically by way of analysing their DNA, it has been considered necessary to keep jigging things around.

As a result, whilst the Lily family used to include onions, garlic, chives and for that matter asparagus, it is now the case that the Lily family only really includes lilies whilst onions, garlic and chives have been moved across to the Amaryllis family and asparagus now have a family all of their own. Linnaeus' almost understandable system has morphed into a huge system that inconveniently keeps changing and shuffling around. As a result, unless you are a botanist, I suggest you don't trouble yourself with the finer details.

On the other hand a basic understanding of how the most common plants you will encounter are grouped together into families can be helpful even for ordinary gardeners like you and me. This is because plants in the same family often share some characteristics. It is helpful to know, for example, that most members of the rose family cope well with clay, or most members of the carrot family flower in the spring, or most members of the brassica family are prone to club root and so on.

Surprisingly, despite the hundreds of plant families that exist, if you garden in the UK and if you garden in a vaguely normal manner, just ten of them will probably account for the larger part of your gardening. You may find it surprises you to see who is related to whom.

The Rose Family – *Rosaceae*	Not just roses, but also cotoneaster, hawthorn and rowan. More surprisingly still the family includes apples, pears, plums, cherries, strawberries, raspberries and even lady's mantle. Most members of the family are tough and most flowers have five petals and most members cope well with clay – my favourite of the plant families!
The Potato Family – *Solanaceae*	Peppers, tomatoes, aubergines, tobacco and, of course, potatoes. Actually there is a killer streak in this exotic family (don't eat green potatoes) because a number of its members have parts which are high in the poison solanine. As a result deadly nightshade is a member and you can see the family resemblance in its leaves. The family also includes petunias and there is even some sort of family likeness there too.
The Mint Family – *Lamiaceae*	Basil! Sage! Thyme! And of course mint. This family has plenty to offer inside and outside the kitchen. The attractive weed 'self-heal' is a member. Distinguished by often aromatic foliage and an ability to really romp given the right conditions.
The Daisy Family – *Compositae*	So much more than daisies. A plant family that has poured itself into plant catalogues and municipal planting schemes with the greatest of gusto; from zinnias to marigolds and from cosmos to sunflowers. However, you may be surprised to hear it includes lettuce, artichoke and tarragon. On the other side of the ledger we have it to thank for thistles and dandelions (not that either trouble me particularly).

The Carrot Family – *Umbelliferae*

This family of plants is responsible for the great sprays of flower you see each spring if you are lucky enough to live near a patch of cow parsley. Many of its members flower in this same extravagant sea spray sort of way (angelica, dill, fennel and even parsley or coriander if you let them). Hemlock is cousin to the humble carrot and famously did for Socrates.

The Mustard Family – *Brassicaceae*

This is the home of your 'greens' – broccoli, Brussels sprouts, cabbage, kale and the like. However, it also houses real garden favourites like candytuft, stocks and perhaps best of all, wallflowers.

The Pea Family – *Leguminosae*

Not just the harbinger of good eating but also of some ecstatically delicate flowers such as sweet peas and lupins. Even the humble bird's foot trefoil, a common weed, has the same delicate and delightful flower shape and I am grateful I have so much of it in the meadow (and lawns) at home.

The Buttercup Family – *Ranunculaceae*

This family is responsible for the ubiquitous weed (beloved by bees as it flowers when little else does) but it reaches very heady heights indeed with clematis, delphiniums and aquilegias. The odd creeping buttercup seems a small price to pay.

The Amaryllis Family – *Amaryllidaceae*

Perhaps the first plant family in this list with a less familiar name. This is one of the greatest of all plant families. In addition to daffodils and snowdrops it includes agapanthus, now a firm garden favourite. Also home to onions, garlic and chives (not hard to see how those three are related).

The Lily Family – *Liliaceae*

Lilies are of course among the most statuesque plants to add to your cutting patch if you like bringing flowers into your house, but they can also be naturalised in grass (snake's head fritillaries) and provide spangle in pots (toad lilies or tulips).

– Weeds –

All of the plant families covered in the previous section have their own contribution to make to the world of weeds; even their desirable members may present as weeds if they seed or creep into the wrong place. As you start your gardening life, and particularly as you start talking to other gardeners, you will come up against the following formula again and again: 'A weed is merely a plant growing in the wrong place'. Whilst this helpfully illustrates the role of gardener as 'curator' it rather misses the universal truth that any garden will have a list of real weeds (not merely desirable escapees).

Actually, grass is a main contender in most gardens because you want a flowerbed not a meadow but in my garden I also grapple with a good number of the standard adversaries: docks, thistles, creeping buttercup, dandelion, herb robert, cleavers and the ones most people dread: bindweed and ground elder. This is a relatively common list but as mentioned every garden will have its own shortlist defined by the particular conditions it offers.

There are of course real specialists like horsetail, and people who encounter it may rue the day they bought a garden with damp patches. Actually horsetail is prehistoric and deserving of awe. It starts life looking like a mushroom and then grows into (I think) quite graceful wands bedecked by needles. The trouble is its root system can travel yards into the soil and you definitely don't want it in your veg patch.

Whilst perennials like horsetail might need more careful thought, most weeds just need pulling. It stands to reason that if you don't pull an annual weed and it sets seed you are giving its offspring a chance they don't deserve.

But some weeds will always slip the net (by definition they are master survivors) and this has to be accepted. Weeding a garden is a bit like trying to lead a kind life; it is certainly possible to improve matters but seemingly impossible to reach perfection. I used to be more of a purist and considered that the aim should be to eradicate every single weed so that even though failure was inevitable it was by the smallest possible margin. Now I take a different approach, I weed just enough to ensure that the weeds don't interfere with the things I am trying to grow; beyond that I don't trouble myself.

In this garden, troublesome perennial weeds like bindweed get stuffed in a bin with water to rot down. Everything else goes on the compost heap or gets deposited in little piles under the foliage of an obliging nearby shrub!

People get in a flap about bindweed and generally speaking it must be taken on. All I can do is speak from experience and tell you I have permanently removed patches of bindweed by giving them a proper going over with a trowel in the spring and then returning to remorselessly pick any little purple shoots that subsequently come up. As you pick these you sometimes find a section of root you missed in the initial assault and these come up in little segments at the base of the material you pull. It is most satisfying. If you keep going in the end you win.

A number of so-called weeds are really just quite beautiful wildflowers. I am indulgent towards marrow and self-heal. Speedwell is an alarmingly beautiful little flower and mouse's ear is lovely too. I love meadow vetchling and bird's foot trefoil. Are these weeds? Farmers probably think so. All cranesbill 'weeds' are essentially geraniums and at the time of writing the jagged-leaved cranesbill in the meadow is lovely. The line between a weed and a flower can be rather fine.

I have never used weedkiller in this garden. The most common one is glyphosate. People say it may be bad for human health but that isn't what stops me. I have turned my back on the whole cohort of chemicals and having come this far I don't intend to stop now. Our drive is a couple of hundred yards long and perhaps twice a year I get on my hands and knees and move down it, weeding. It takes me all of a few hours. This is the price I pay to be chemical free and I am happy to pay it. The drive isn't littered with weeds. Sometimes I break my own rules and leave a sprig of something attractive here or there.

One organic compromise is to use a flamethrower. I particularly dislike the noise they make and whilst I accept that they speed matters up, at the end of the day there is nothing like pulling a weed by its roots to truly arrest its development! The other great trick up an organic gardener's sleeve, when it comes to annual weeds, is to use a mulch. Anything that provides a physical barrier will stop annual weeds growing: lengths of old carpet, landscape fabric, woodchips or a thick covering of compost. A hoe can be useful too, particularly if you keep it sharp.

My final tip would be to say that you should never underestimate the value of a midwinter weed. Everyone says there is nothing to do in the garden in winter and this is complete nonsense. Winter is a brilliant time to weed provided the soil isn't waterlogged. Weeding is just another slice of the joy of gardening – try to actively enjoy it.

– *Concluding Part I* –

Hopefully you have decided to leave perfect lawns to the Oxbridge colleges and instead to take appropriate pride in what will become a far more interesting and varied 'green space' than any grass monoculture could be. You have also come to see the local plant nursery not merely as a place that incubates young plants, but a place that can incubate young gardeners too. The difference between acid and alkali soil is no longer a mystery and in fact you know as much about soil as most gardeners do including that we all strive for loam, that mixture of the better qualities of both sand and clay. And you know the most important thing of all, that this is always achieved by adding organic matter.

You have started, or you shortly will start, pottering about with seeds and compost and plant labels – there really is nothing quite so enjoyable – and even if you are furnishing a single window box, the pleasure is just the same. I strongly suspect that, as your first little crop of seedlings emerge from the dark compost a new sap of hope will rise within your heart too. You have a growing sense that plants belong to families and many of their tribes will now be familiar to you from your trips to the plant nursery.

Starting out on a new garden adventure is one of the most exciting things that can be done (I think so anyway) and you are still well within the honeymoon period so enjoy all the new smells, sounds, sights and discoveries. Hold your hopes for your own patch tightly and don't listen to any naysayers. If the sum total of your commitment to your garden thus far is reading this book you are already a gardener in spirit and I would like, on behalf of all gardeners, to extend a very warm welcome to you.

Part II

Becoming your own garden designer

– Boundaries –

Having already discussed a reasonably large number of plants and their management we are now going to think for the first time about the garden as a whole; in other words, we are becoming garden designers. There are generally considered to be two types of gardening enthusiast. Some people are driven by a simple love of plants (these people are often called plantswomen and plantsmen) and their gardens often have very little design and are really just about growing as many different plants as possible. Other people are driven not so much by a love of plants as a love of design (these are the garden designers) and whilst they might like plants very much, the plants represent an opportunity to paint a bigger picture still.

Speaking personally, I am not sure I am principally driven either by a love of plants or of good design, but rather the way these elements speak to the mystery of place. For me a garden is about bringing a pre-existing sense of a place exquisitely into focus. What drove me to create Skymeadow (my garden at home) was a sort of yearning for, and a desire to celebrate, the sense of place that already existed here. For example I chose cherry trees for my avenue because I felt they better echoed the essential softness of the countryside in which my garden happens to sit. But had I lived within a dramatic escarpment I might have played a different game.

However, for a place to exist it must be distinguishable from other places and this is why the concept of a boundary really is at the root of any meaningful discussion of any garden. In fact, from the earliest times the words used in most languages for a garden have simply meant an enclosed space. Adam and Eve were in paradise, itself from the Persian word meaning 'enclosure'. Our own word garden comes from Anglo-Saxon 'gardo' which means 'enclosed'. Large or small, a garden is an enclosure and it should work as such. So the first thing to do with any new garden, or an existing one you wish to improve, is to walk the boundary and really look. Do you need to plant things out, or cut things back or create portholes to the outside world? A boundary can be playful, but a garden with no boundary is no garden at all. Once your boundary is in place, even if it is merely in your mind's eye, you have a garden.

– Starting to think about paths –

What follows from the idea of a garden as an enclosure is that it must be traversable. How are we to move around this enclosed place? All gardens will in fact have pre-existing paths. Any garden (forecourt, parking lot or field for that matter) has its own natural ones. Only time and use will reveal them, but given the topography of any particular space the majority of humans, if asked to cross it, will usually elect to use the same route. We are just like badgers and other animals who beat the same earth across the same country into their own visible thoroughfares. These natural highways and byways should not be ignored, because otherwise you will have an expensive path that remains unused on one hand and muddy grooves across your flowerbeds on the other!

There are some basic rules with paths. Every path needs to have an intended destination (rather than being built out of the general feeling the garden needs a path) and every path will ideally take someone to something, and preferably back again. Of course the practical benefit to a path is safe transit during winter when all around is wet and muddy. But at some point you will start to make aesthetic decisions too. How wide do you want the path to be? It is a fine thing to have a path that two people can walk down side by side, or even hand in hand. Equally, there is an intimacy to a narrow pass. A path, being a decent metaphor we must imagine for life

61

generally, can have great romance. Straight paths encourage brisk walking whereas a meandering curling path will encourage meandering in those who use it. Do you want a fast formal pace, or a slow gentle one?

Paths must lead somewhere but this doesn't necessarily mean to a garden shed. A path might lead to a particularly good view, to a place that is shaded from the midsummer sun or past a notable contour. Of course, as you are now all gardeners, you will appreciate that paths are also viewing platforms for your precious plants. Tall plants work well at a turn because they invite the traveller to consider them and wonder what might lie beyond. Low growing clumps of lovely *Gypsophila*, or even a patch of wild violets, can soften the straight edge of a path. Do you want plants spilling on to the path? I generally do. Do you want plants in the path? I generally do.

I absolutely love brick paths, but they are expensive and time consuming to make. I don't mind gravel paths though I prefer a hard surface underfoot to a squelchy one. Stepping stones can make a very good solution because they are cheaper than both brick and gravel but they are useless if you are pushing a wheelbarrow! The same applies to wooden sleepers.

Remember, a rudimentary path is no more than trampled grass. Paths can absolutely be established by simply cutting a strip. In many ways these are my favourite types of path because every year (or even every time you mow) you can make little adjustments to improve them.

– Starting to think about hedges –

If the first use for a hedge is to enclose your garden, its second use is to mark out the various rooms within it. Of course, walls and fences (which really, for our purposes, are just forms of hedge) may have their role in this process too; but neither will do much to help wildlife. Hedges can be used to play with perspective; for example a path running between two hedges will appear longer the closer the two hedges are to each other. Equally, you can use a hedge to play with scale; the larger a hedge is, the smaller and more snug will appear the space that it encloses.

Hedges can be sharp and formal or soft and irregular and as such can lend a distinct mood to the part of the garden in which they grow. To my mind far too many are sharp and formal. To provide an exciting flourish, two ends of a hedge can be allowed to grow together into an archway and deliver a real and pleasing sense of permanence to a garden. How many people have a gate through a hedge that could be allowed to develop into an archway but never think to let it happen? In my opinion most garden hedges could usually be a little taller. After lengthy deliberation and much trial and error I have settled on eight feet as the general go-to height for hedging in this garden.

A single species hedge will always look more formal than a mixed species hedge. In the countryside hedges that start out as single species will gain a new species, it is reckoned, every hundred years. The number of species a country hedge contains is generally considered a reasonable way of dating it, so a mixed hedge with hawthorn, dog rose, elder and elm might be reckoned four hundred years old.

In earlier times (and even today) hedges have been used to create impermeable barriers to defend settlements. If you want to improve security you clearly need to choose something spiky. Whatever else they are, hedges are far more than just a handy way to obscure a neighbour's garage. The hedges you plant will have a greater impact on your garden, probably, than any other intervention so give them the level of consideration they deserve.

– Learning to look –

In my last book, *Skymeadow: Notes from an English Gardener*, I wrote at some length about my approach to garden design and how it seems to be upside down when compared to how most people go about it. Most people start with the human and ask themselves what they want from their garden. I start at the other end. I start with the garden and ask what can be done to help it become more fully itself? I would urge you, in the first instance, not to just bring your garden a long list of what you want but rather to spend time in it and see what it might be prepared to yield. This means properly looking.

We have an area where the children play on swings and a climbing frame, a place where we barbeque, a place to sit and watch water, another for fruit growing and of course vegetable and herb growing. We also have favourite spots for sleeping on a rug on the grass in the summer and so the list goes on. But all these places have emerged, somehow, as gifts from the garden itself, not because I have imposed myself on it. In fact, without exception, when I have forced solutions they have always failed.

Cultivate the ability not just to see but to look. A long, patient and deep look at the garden is what is required. Look calmly and intently like a wild beast of the Serengeti prospecting for lunch. If you are anything like me it will have to be quiet too, because as soon as there is any noise my ability to look deeply and properly evaporates. Get a sense of the roll of the land so you can hover over it in your mind's eye. Think about the arc of the sun; the run of the wind through it, and the sense of place it already has. My most successful garden interventions really have come from bringing some quality, some thing the garden already had, more to the fore rather than hoping to replicate some cheap thrill torn from the pages of a garden magazine. I have tried both, of course.

– *Gardens should run green with sap* –

At least that is what gardens ought to do providing they haven't been smothered under concrete and decking. The line between how much hard and soft landscaping to have is very fine indeed. I find large areas swamped with concrete and decking austere and somewhat depressing. They are the sad evidence of humanity's attempt to better nature; and they never do. On the other hand the fact that carefully sited paths, terraces and walls can be the difference between an excellent garden and an average one is hard to argue with. Essentially I think this comes down to ratio.

Too much hard landscaping is in some way hubristic. It says that nature is to be obliterated by our will. In some settings this urge to conquer or even dominate can be aesthetically pleasing. After all, it is man cast as genius, the talented child of creation who can do almost anything he wishes, that led to our expedition to the moon. But in truth apart from Neil Armstrong's spacecraft and spacesuit he was surrounded by the unknowable extremities of space and plunged into an austere environment; in other words the ratio was there. It wasn't man obliterating but man heroic. On the other hand a small suburban garden surrounded by a chemically treated wooden fence with only decking and concrete for a floor is not man as hero but man as obliterator. When you are standing in that garden there is no ratio.

When I started I had grandiose plans for walls and paths, lots of both, a relatively comprehensive smothering in fact. I got very excited about building a walled garden and almost started it but as I paced it out for the final time to check my calculations prior to ordering the bricks I suddenly thought, 'What am I doing?'

An evergreen hedge would still block the view of the vegetable garden from the house, it would provide a better barrier to wind and provide bed and breakfast for birds. I checked myself. Even though I was planning on building it myself the project would have swallowed a huge amount of resource in both time and money and it just didn't seem to serve any of the overarching objectives of the garden (chiefly to be a nature reserve that surprises and delights). After the walled garden experience I stopped longing for bricks in the way I used to. Now I think far more fondly of the endlessly fascinating patina of a green environment, particularly an evergreen one.

Hard landscaping has an incredibly important role to play, and can undoubtedly transform a garden but I now try to use soft landscaping where I can. These are the sorts of decisions in a garden that keep sap rising. But sap won't rise without water.

– Butts, ponds and hosepipes –

Water comes from the sky, soaks into the ground and is then released back into the sky (slowly) by plants. Plants with thick leathery leaves, the succulents and evergreens, have evolved to hold on to water well so that it transpires slowly, whereas a small violet will wilt in a matter of moments if its water supply is arrested through, for example, having been recently picked.

Nonetheless all plants take water from the ground and give it back to the sky and all skies gift water to the ground (unless you happen to be in a desert, in which case your gardening options are severely limited). The more I garden the more I see the whole show as being indelibly tied to this essential process. An alien looking down might well conclude that as a species we are no more than rather noisy freeloaders attached like limpets to the movement of water between sky and earth; certainly most of our food is dependent on this cycle.

We garden in what is considered to be the driest corner of England – the east of East Anglia – and this has taught me to respect water. Without it (and we frequently don't have nearly enough) the most carefully laid plans unravel. In fact, if I was starting again, I would think more seriously about water at the outset. I might even have strategically positioned bodies of water throughout the garden. I might yet.

That said, I garden quite hard. No plant is particularly coddled. Once a plant is established it might benefit from some weeding at its base and a mulch in spring but it might not and generally speaking it is on its own. Certainly I do not provide all the plants in this garden with a weekly soak. I *do* water vegetables because otherwise you get a desultory crop and I *do* water newly planted babies and trees during the summer in their first few seasons because otherwise they often die. The trouble for me is that, despite my best intentions, some enthusiasm always gets the better of me during the winter and the garden is always chock-full of babies the following spring.

When our summers include rain everything grows but when they don't (and they increasingly don't) all growth stops and I end up getting hot and flustered carrying water about. For several years I had a somewhat restricted water supply and the flow rate at our house never rose above eleven litres a minute. This would be fine for a normal domestic environment but was incredibly frustrating for me! I can't express how hard it made our long dry eastern summers given the scale of the garden I was attempting to establish. Despite various countermeasures (like strategically placing plastic drums in the centre of the garden and filling them up with water in advance) it still took me two whole days to water the garden. All this is now a long distant memory but I still feel pinched by the experience. It has had a lasting impact on how I think about the role of water in gardens.

Eventually, we were able to install a borehole. There is a significant risk with geology because whilst there is usually local evidence related to nearby boreholes, you never really know until you get down there. When it comes to drawing water in this part of England you ought to be able to, because you will eventually make the chalk aquifer, but eventually that might mean a great many metres and each metre has a cost! We got there in the end, but whilst the drill rig operators and contractors were professional and calm throughout I was like a wobbling jelly, desperate to get hourly progress reports! I can now draw one litre of pure lovely water a second. It is no exaggeration to say that water had been the missing ingredient in this garden.

Water butts are fashionable and there are good reasons for this. They are eco friendly, the water they provide isn't laced with chlorine, it is free and best of all rainwater tends to be slightly acidic which means it is better for watering those ericaceous plants you are growing in pots (heather, rhododendrons, azaleas etc). Despite all these advantages I have found they have one drawback too: they encourage mosquitoes and as a result I got rid of one because it was positioned just outside our kitchen in an area where we often sit. Whilst mosquitoes don't seem to manage to get through my leathery skin the one thing we have in common is that they are exceptionally fond of my wife.

Of course you don't have a huge amount of choice when it comes to positioning water butts because ordinarily speaking they need to be close to a roof, which means next to a house or shed. Having said that, I have heard of people designing systems with considerable lengths of piping that move water from the roof of the house off to various water butts and then beyond in order to cover their whole gardens. Whilst this would be impossible in my garden (not enough roof, too much garden) if I lived in a town and had an average size rear garden I think I would construct something along these lines; creating a borehole of the sky is a very attractive idea.

If I could afford to have standpipes all over the garden (and if I didn't mind trenching through now established parts of it) I would but I don't want to spend the money nor do the trenching so watering here still involves super-long lengths of hosepipe. As you navigate a hosepipe through a garden it is all too easy to bend or snap plant stems with the slack as you turn a corner. Avoid this by plunging sticks (or sturdy bamboo canes) at the turns as you go. Incidentally it is now possible to get long hosepipes that shrink when you turn the tap off. This is a great solution that removes the need to endlessly loop them up against something.

Even with the borehole (or perhaps because of it) I remain interested in extending a network of waterways through the garden down into the valley which would not only immeasurably increase the garden's horticultural potential, hugely increase its usefulness to insects, be breathtakingly beautiful but also, if planned carefully, play a wider part in an effort to irrigate this rain-starved hillside. However, this would be a very major project indeed so it is currently sitting on the top shelf gathering dust. Whichever way you cut it there are three critical considerations when growing plants: water, light and heat. Of the three water is the only one you can truly hope to have any real control over, so it is essential to think it through at the outset.

– Organic can equal easy –

There are sound and selfless reasons to garden organically but the very best reasons are entirely selfish. I find that organic gardening is just easier. The plants you grow are healthy and happier; better to look at, better to eat and you don't have to waste all that time spraying. It is worth considering the general principles of organic gardening at the design stage so you can fully reap its rewards later. After five years of running an entirely organic operation chemicals look increasingly to me like no more than quick and tenuous fixes. Kill one pest (and who knows what else with it) but it will shortly be back, or something else will. Then what? Kill it again? This all stacks up to quite a large number of interventions. Surely better to create the conditions in which the chemicals are not needed in the first place?

When we first got here we had terrible aphids in the newly dug rose garden, though it is worth saying that the sappy new growth most young plants throw out is a particular attraction to aphids. I went to the shed and picked up a can of spray that had come from London and as I walked down to the rose garden I just thought, 'What are you doing?' So I took the spray back to the shed and instead resolved to make every possible effort to welcome aphids' natural predators to Skymeadow, principally ladybirds and lacewings. I now leave everything standing in the rose garden until the first lick of warmth in the spring to provide these insects with winter quarters (tidying everything in the autumn and then again in the spring is pointless anyway). I grow plenty of lavender, rosemary and artichoke, all of which seem to be ladybird favourites. All insects like long grass so I make sure I have plenty of that too. I don't even allow anyone to sweep ladybirds from the window frames in the house, and preserve a good few thousand that way! Now we have hardly any aphids. Better still, I think because the roses aren't weakened by either aphids or by the spray necessary to remove them, they don't now get much black spot. Many people would spray for aphids and then spray for black spot. I don't have to do either job. Organic really can equal easy.

Other organic principles have benefited the rose garden too. At the outset I knew I shouldn't create a monoculture, that is to say plant a large group of a single plant. Nature rarely throws monocultures out and all monocultures, whether they are of rose, box or cabbage are an invitation to create a reservoir of disease. Also, I don't overfeed our roses because overfeeding (with artificial fertilisers, which are expensive and time consuming to apply) encourages the soft sappy growth aphids love. All our roses are fed only by way of an early spring mulch which contains plenty of muck. This also helpfully covers over any diseased leaf litter from the previous season, further curtailing black spot. But despite all this, I put the health of the rose garden principally down to ladybirds!

What happens in nature is that populations of birds, insects and even fungi self-regulate. If you remove one so-called trouble species entirely you just make a gap for a new competitor species and you end up with a see-saw effect and happy agrochemical companies. Whereas if you set conditions to favour insects and birds generally (plenty of water, season round pollen, plenty of shelter, plenty of native foliage and – of course – no poison) then the see-saw boom and bust cycle that demands intervention is replaced by a situation in which everything is there but nothing (you hope) gets out of hand.

So when you design your garden why not design in thickets of long grass and specific plants to encourage natural aphid predators? If you plant a rose garden plan to have lots of other plants in it too. One stitch now saves nine later. Given that you will want to feed your plants in a natural slow release sort of way you are going to need lots of compost, so include a composting station at the outset. And there is nothing like introducing some water to turbo charge the health of an insect population in a garden, so think about space for a pond. All those extra insects will drive pollination in your vegetable bed too. Organic gardening is all about establishing a giant virtuous circle and it is much more fun.

Finally, I think neatness itself has a lot to answer for. This year I had thousands of opium poppies spring up in the vegetable garden. Rather than weed every one for neatness's sake (as I might have done in earlier years) I just removed blocks of them when I wanted to plant something. One recent block was for lettuce. After a few weeks I noticed not a single lettuce plant had been troubled by a slug. As I cleared another block of opium poppies for some spinach I found a thousand little slugs feasting away on them. It's a good idea not to take every single weed from your cold frames for the same reason. Tidiness, beyond a certain point, is a sort of tyranny. If you jettison it you will halve your garden maintenance and boost your organic credentials. It is remarkable how often the two concepts run in tandem. The only truly low maintenance garden is no garden at all; but I suspect the battle for an easy garden that is still worthy of the name will be won mostly in your mind.

– *Concluding Part II* –

No doubt as you have read this section your mind has been hovering over your own patch. Squaring away your boundaries, making a conscious effort to properly look and ensuring you have a ready supply of water is fairly universal to any garden project but I suspect you have also started to make decisions, or at least highlight decisions, that are unique to your circumstances.

These decisions may include overarching strategic objectives about what purpose your garden might serve. If the military pride their ability to shock and awe, I pride my ability to surprise and delight and I don't think this is possible in a garden without wildlife. A garden without wildlife is a bit like one of those stately homes without a family. It can be beautiful and even worth visiting but it is somehow eerie, it lacks movement. I don't want my garden to be merely a symbol of my ability to carpet bomb with bedding plants and slug pellets. I want slugs and I want the birds that eat them!

Different parts of my garden are infused with different, often quite personal, meaning. But there are of course perfectly legitimate objectives that are more simple. Some people might just want their garden to support their house aesthetically, or they might want to take on what is essentially a rewilding project with little organised horticulture, or achieve a level of formality that is appropriate to entertaining large numbers of people, or build an Italian garden, or a Japanese one for that matter.

Whatever you choose, it is helpful to have some sense of what you are trying to achieve at the outset. However, I hope, above all, you now have a sense that all this planning can be done in some sort of partnership with the garden itself. It doesn't just happen at the kitchen table with coloured pencils. It happens through being in your garden and really looking and considering what your garden might be prepared to yield. Finally, I hope you will also consider laying out an organic system at the outset, not just for the selfless reasons but for the selfish ones too.

Part III

Thinking like a gardener

– *A gardener's calendar* –

We will start, where any gardener should, on the shortest day. There are two definitions of winter, meteorological winter and astronomical winter. Meteorological winter refers unsurprisingly to the three coldest months (December, January and February) and is the definition most commonly used. Astronomical winter refers to the three months that fall immediately after the shortest day, also known as the winter solstice. The winter solstice usually falls on the 21st or 22nd of December though it can fall on the 20th or 23rd – but whatever day it falls on it is the true starting gun for the garden.

Whilst it will be months before everything is in full swing the days are getting longer and even if you don't notice them doing so the birds will. Their song picks up remarkably quickly after the celestial clock passes annual midnight. The table below shows you what might be expected to flower from the shortest day on. I am going to introduce you to eighty-odd plants. Whilst this might sound like a frightening number, I bet you are capable of readily identifying a good number of them, perhaps more than half, already. When you think there are many hundreds of thousands of plants the world over, it is surprising also to think that a passing acquaintance with under a hundred plants will give you the confidence necessary to walk round most people's gardens and have something to say!

Of course, when any given plant will flower can change year to year under the influence of varying weather conditions. Also, things can flower for long periods but really find their feet in the garden at a particular moment. For example little sprigs of forget-me-nots can be found flowering in this garden for most of the season, but it is the great early carpet supporting the tulips that gives them their moment to really shine. Equally salvias will start flowering in May but it is their contribution in August and September which is most notable to me. So the table below isn't so much a hard and fast guide as a reflection of what plant I might be looking for at any given moment in the year. Even when not in flower many plants more than pay their way for the rest of the year with their foliage.

December	Viburnum	Winter-flowering Honeysuckle	Winter-flowering Clematis
January	Christmas Box	Hamamelis	Winter Aconite	Cyclamen	Snowdrops	Christmas Roses
February	Winter Irises	Anemone	Muscari	Crocuses	Mahonia	Forsythia
March	Oriental Quince	Hyacinth	Rosemary	Primroses	Snake's Head Fritillaries	Daffodils	Daphnes	Blossom
April	Blossom	Dog's tooth Violets	Flowering Currants	Forget-me-nots	Tulips	Wallflowers	Primulas	Bleeding Heart	Bergenias	Crown Imperials	Lily of the Valley	Bluebells
May	Cow Parsley	Lilacs	Laburnum	Wisteria	Aquilegias	Ajuga	Alliums	Mexican Orange Blossom	Californian Lilac	Peonies	Geums	Summer-flowering Irises	Lupins	Early Honeysuckle
June	Roses	Poppies	Summer-flowering Clematis	Foxgloves	Love-in-a-mist	Freesias	Snapdragons	Geraniums	Sweet Peas	Pinks	Linaria	Lilies	Lavender
July	Delphiniums	Pelargoniums	Cornflowers	Marigolds	Gladioli	Mock Orange	Later-flowering Honeysuckle	Later-flowering Clematis

August	Buddleia I Sunflowers I Hollyhocks I Sea Hollies I Red Hot Pokers I Crocosmia I Artichokes I Verbena bonariensis I Salvias
September	Dahlias I Japanese Anemone I Agapanthus I Nasturtiums I Cosmos I Sedums I Rudbeckia I Autumn Crocuses
October	First frost, fall back on berries, hips and fruit
November	First frost, fall back on berries, hips and fruit

– Planting –

Planting is generally considered its own department within garden design and other than ensuring the plants you acquire are of good quality there are really two aspects to it: the physical act of putting plants into the ground and the imaginative act of deciding which ones to use.

Sometimes garden designers are hired just to provide a planting plan for a single flowerbed. They ought to consider how much sun and rain it is likely to get, how sheltered it is and the condition of the soil it contains. They will also consider seasonal interest and what the client has said they want. Armed with this information they will deliver a planting plan (the gardening version of a map for the flowerbed) and then tip up on planting day to ensure the plants that have been ordered are of good quality and that they are planted correctly.

For better or worse, this is not really how I have gone about things. I 'saw' a rose garden, then I 'saw' a snaking sweet pea bed, then I 'saw' a scruffy flowerbed by the barn with lots of foxgloves (and I have probably 'seen' far too many other things over the years) but once I 'see' something I then tend to start digging and planting my way through until it, or something approximating it, emerges.

However you go about it, the most common cause of failure is that the plants used don't correlate well to the conditions in which they are planted. For example, it is a bad idea to plant hydrangeas along a south facing wall in an already dry bed, or to plant roses in a miserly thin soil or lavender in a swamp. The second most common reason for failure is that when plants arrive they appear rather small, but of course if things go according to plan they have a habit of getting quite a lot larger over time.

Here are a few basic tips for getting plants in the ground:

Basic positioning

You won't get a pelargonium to flower in the shade of an oak tree. Whilst this is obviously hyperbolic, if you have a plant that wants full sun (and the plant label will generally tell you) don't plant it behind a thumping great (usually perennial) neighbour.

Another basic but effective general piece of advice is to plant either single specimens or in groups of three, five, seven or nine. There is a poetry in numbers and an arrangement of two or four will never look quite so good as three or five.

It is always a good idea to position plants in their pots where they are to be planted before actually digging the holes so that you can make little adjustments before, rather than after, they are in the ground. As with school photographs, the larger ones generally go to the back.

Most plants need more space not less

As a rule plants benefit from being laid out with more rather than less space between them. It is always tempting to think that stuffing more in will equal a better display, but the last thing you want is a row of half-grown anaemic plants competing with each other and getting nowhere in particular.

Obviously it is a question of balance. The plant label should give you a guide, but I have come to the general conclusion of erring on the side of giving them more rather than less space.

Get the size of the planting hole right

Dig the hole before you even attempt to take the plant from the pot. Make sure the hole is bigger than the pot (if necessary use the pot itself to check). What you are attempting to avoid is removing the plant from the pot, half planting it only to discover the hole is too shallow, removing it to who knows where, re-digging, retrieving it and stuffing it in again. I have of course done all these things myself but it is definitely not best practice.

Gentle movements

Hold the pot with one hand and cup the other over the soil with a few fingers on either side of the stem. Gently turn the pot upside down and watch the plant slither out. Tap if necessary. It may sound obvious, but do this as close as possible to the planting hole. If necessary, you can usually gently pull woody things out by their stems but if it is green and sappy you must be careful not to touch the stem for fear of damaging it.

Burying

Because you dug a big enough hole in the first place there is now plenty of spoil to hand. Mass the spoil up against the plant's roots, more than looks necessary, then firmly but not violently press the soil and roots down, if possible in a single action. I sometimes clench my fist and use my knuckles to do this.

You want to get contact between the pot soil and the ground soil, without air bubbles and preferably without crushing the roots in the process. This is also why it's important to always water generously at planting time, even if it is raining, because the water plays its part in removing any large air pockets that may have formed below soil.

Horticultural grit

Some plants will easily rot if left in heavy wet soil over winter. Frankly I plant almost all bulbs and tubers on a bed of grit and most other things too. Particularly because we garden on clay, I adhere to the general policy: if in doubt plant on a few inches of grit.

Drought precautions

I generally create a ridge of soil in a circle or square around the base of the plant after I have put it into the ground. This is to ensure what little rain we have doesn't run off and instead is focused towards the roots of the plant as they grow. If you live in the wet west this may not be necessary.

Incidentally, once plants are in the ground I am a great believer of checking the forecast and watering them in advance of a spell of clement weather so they can make the most of it when it comes, turning as much of the sun as possible into growth. If faced with a sudden burst of heat and light but no moisture at their toes some plants will shut down into a sort of survival mode, anticipating a period of drought.

– *Some thoughts on colour* –

I think people worry too much about colour, or rather they worry about colour in the wrong way. It is true that certain colour combinations do seem to clash but what might be considered an out and out clash in the eyes of one observer could be the very elixir of visual excitement for another.

Certain colour combinations will deliver a sense of drama and energy whilst others will have a generally calming effect and as with painting, a small brush delivering lots of little strokes (wildflower meadow) will have quite a different effect on mood to a large brush delivering a single block of colour (municipal planting scheme).

Painters use a colour wheel (which has all the different shades of colour merging into one another in a circle) and it has long been known that shades that sit near each other on the wheel will create a sense of harmony, whereas shades that are opposite each other will startle. But rather than fretting about the risk of colour clashes it is more profitable to try to think of colour in the round, and specifically how it can affect the mood of a particular corner of the garden.

Here are some basic tips:

- Soft pastel shades are generally calming, jumbling them up rarely offends and can provide an expansive calming effect (like a wildflower meadow).

- Bright colours are generally arresting and exciting and jumbling them up can be risky and deliver an almost violent, jarring effect.
- Using soft pastel shades to support a single bright colour can be a wise step (as with poppies in a wildflower meadow).
- Red is clearly hot and energetic and sometimes even aggressive; yellow and orange can deliver heat without so much insistence and aggression.
- White is very useful to highlight other colours, especially the greens, silvers and greys of foliage.
- Large stretches of a single colour can be impressive if executed well and dull if executed badly.
- Light colours tend to glow in the evening and can even brighten shadier spots in a garden. Darker colours tend to have the effect of shading, as with doing a pencil sketch.

I am increasingly convinced that we all fail to properly consider the range, scope and splendour of green, nor do we appreciate how satisfying a massed array of different greens can be. We are hardwired to love green. As a species we likely developed the ability to see it when we became farmers and it probably conferred an evolutionary advantage in terms of assessing pasture. I certainly can't get enough of it. The range of different shades of green in the average garden is staggering if you just stop and take it in; yellow greens, silver greens, blue greens, grey greens, red greens, acid greens (and many, many other greens besides). I suspect this is why painters often say they find green a hard colour to mix.

This is the moment to point out that thinking about scent is just as important as thinking about colour and here fun can be had too. Why not dedicate the area where you like to sit out on a summer's evening to plants that have evolved to flower and smell at night? These plants take advantage of moths for pollination and unsurprisingly include evening primrose but also tobacco plants, jasmines and certain honeysuckles. The point is that scent can build mood just as colour can.

– *Wildlife as spectacle* –

It is the end of May and I have just looked out of my study window and seen the first red admiral butterfly sunning itself on the gravel. Yesterday I saw the first peacock. Three days ago as I turned the compost heap I saw a puss moth, so named because of its extraordinary cat-like fur. Birds too come and visit through the different quarters of the year. The sound of the first cuckoo, the sight of the first swift or a chance encounter with some other long distance traveller all build suspense and deliver visual impact. Creatures build spectacle just as plants do. It is worth thinking about wildlife in these terms.

One morning a year ago I opened the door to my study and spooked many tribes of songbird from the four or so bird feeders in the snaking sweet pea bed which curls around the south side of the house. A charm of goldfinches, a zephyr of long-tailed tits, and a quarrel of sparrows (along with a goodly number of great tits, coal tits and blue tits, whose collective nouns, if they have them, I don't know) took off in unison, a hundred little fluttering birds of various hues made every which way for the encircling assortment of shrubs, trees and hedgerow (birds like to move from cover to food and back again, so this much, at least, was deliberate). I froze mesmerised and they all seemed to melt back again into their previous positions, as if they had collectively taken a breath in and then out again.

That morning I witnessed a thousand-step ballet playing out before my eyes for the price of a few bags of seed. The overall movement held a pattern in its execution that startled and pleased me in a way that defies clear communication. The best gardens will carry surprise and delight well beyond photosynthesis. A bird feeder in a flowerbed provides season round interest too.

When feeding birds there are a few basic tips. Peanuts will attract many birds as will fatty suet and a general seed mix but goldfinches, for example, will only generally come to Niger seed. A simple goldfinch is among the most exotic sights available in England and the flutter of their gold and scarlet upon the dark green of an evergreen background is a joy. Who wouldn't want to attract them?

You need to be careful with peanuts; never feed birds mouldy ones as this can kill them, and in the spring during the breeding season only ever feed peanuts through a wire mesh because fed individually they will choke the fledglings. Birds can catch diseases off one another (as is the way with humans) and so providing several different feeding stations is a way of cutting down this danger. Washing bird feeders periodically is a good idea too. Don't forget birds like to drink so a bird bath is a solid investment for any garden, particularly one without a pond.

– *A little more on roses* –

The rose is not only a very English symbol, it is a very Catholic one too, with the tradition of the church using the rose as a symbol for Mary 'rose without thorns'. Elizabeth I took a rose as her symbol which presumably by association was intended to underscore her virginity. Of course the House of Lancaster and the House of York had already laid claim to a rose each, the first red and the second white. From a gardening perspective, however, the rose is more or less ideal; it is both delicate and bold. It smells. Its foliage looks great. It takes rough handling. What's not to like?

The history of the rose as a plant in England is more than a little complicated. But here is the basic story. The Elizabethans had a much more reduced palette of roses to use in their gardens than we do. They had the species roses native to the UK. Species roses are the original wild roses from which cultivated ones are bred. So they would have had the dog rose (my favourite of all roses) because it grew in their hedgerows as it does in ours, and they would have had the briar rose which is much the same as the dog rose but its leaves when rubbed smell of apple.

In addition to the native species or wild roses they would have had Alba roses (as per the white rose of York) and Gallica roses (as per the red rose of Lancaster). But all these roses would have flowered only once in the year. There would have been Damask roses too and these were probably the only remontant type available, meaning that they were the only rose at the time capable of flowering more than once in a season.

Then, in the middle of the seventeenth century, Centifolia (so called because they have a hundred petals) emerged from the Netherlands. At the end of the eighteenth century the China roses arrived and the Tea-scented Chinas. Suddenly it was possible to breed between old European and Asian gene pools. New types came thick and fast including Noisette. They had interesting and special qualities including, thanks to the eastern DNA, an improved capacity to flower through-out the season.

Various grandchildren were bred with their grandparents, who were themselves the product of crosses between cousins and soon the average rose had a more detailed pedigree than the average European aristocrat, though was perhaps a little more inbred. Out of this cauldron, sometime in the nineteenth century, the Hybrid Perpetual was born.

To step over further very complex rose breeding matters, which were probably equally incestuous, by the end of the nineteenth century Hybrid Teas had arrived as a further itera-tion and many had names you would recognise from a quick walk around the rose section of a modern nursery, such as Peace.

The early twentieth century saw the arrival of Floribundas and barring a few quirks here and there the next huge impact on the genetics of the rose family would come when David Austin set up shop in the 1960s. He developed The English Rose which is as good as its own type. There are other quirky backwaters of rose DNA. The polyanthas were popular with the Victorians and have fallen out of fashion rather and shrub roses aren't roses that will shrub out nicely, but simply roses that can't be placed into any of the neat categories mentioned above.

To be honest I have spent a fair amount of time thinking about roses and their lineages and I don't fully understand the landscape myself. The above is a working guide but if you want more there are books by rosarians aplenty.

If you want to obscure an ugly shed a rose could be just the ticket, but they will also break up a boring lawn, clamber over an arch or sit as a standard formally in a pot on either side of an entrance. At Sissinghurst rather than removing dead trees Vita Sackville-West ran climbing roses up them to great effect. A rose catalogue is itself a thing of great beauty, but can leave you feeling confused, so what follows, I hope, might give you a head start.

– Roses to scramble or soar –

There is nothing so splendid as a rose vertical. We all know how a rose growing up the side of a cottage can complete the aesthetic sense of dingly-dell well-being but many roses are really prepared to romp and can be used not only to adorn the wall of a cottage but to grow into a tree or even cover the façade of a stately home. Roses that are prepared to grow vertically fall into two categories – 'climbers' and 'ramblers'. The distinction between the two is largely academic other than to note that ramblers will flower only once and they will, as the name suggests, grow more vigorously. They also tend to be highly disease resistant. Climbers on the other hand are more likely to be repeat flowering and also more likely to be kept neatly climbing as opposed to uproariously rambling.

Before we launch in, all roses should be deadheaded. However, if you are doing this in a serious manner to encourage more flowering (as opposed to just a quick tidy) you have to be ruthless and snap off any bloom, even pretty ones, that seem even vaguely on the turn. The minute the plant begins to set seed hormones will foreclose the show. It is also worth mentioning that any rose that has its branches tied at horizontal, or just below, will think it is dying and produce more blooms. This may seem like psychological torture but it is a surprisingly useful piece of information and not just for climbing roses; there is nothing to stop you tying down branches on a rose in the border and I sometimes use little stakes or sticks to do just that.

White

Finding a really good white climbing rose is not an entirely straightforward task. David Austin have bred **Claire Austen** which has the benefit of tolerating north facing walls and also has a good fragrance. The other classic choice would be **Iceberg**, a fine rose and whilst sometimes a bit spindly to start with it will look impressive over time providing an abundance of handsome foliage and true white flowers though not much in the way of fragrance. Both of these white roses are repeat flowering and both will grow to ten to twelve feet or so in height.

Red

It is okay to like a plant, or at least first meet a plant, because you are drawn to a name. With my O'Flaherty forebears, or perhaps merely the idea of them, I admit it was the romance of the name that first drew me to **Dublin Bay** but if you want a solid blood red climber to make a good few feet in height you need look no further. I haven't grown a large red climber in this garden yet, but if I was to I would look at **Étoile de Hollande** for the front of a house or perhaps **Crimson Glory** for a large pergola.

Yellow

Although perhaps unfortunately named, **Golden Showers** is a very popular yellow climber and performs solidly. It is a good choice for a wall if you want a proper golden yellow colour, for example to look well against a black boarded barn. If you see a yellow climber in someone else's garden and ask if it's Golden Showers the answer very frequently is affirmative which will give you an aura of gardening knowledge that might outreach the reality. **Gloire de Dijon** is a more classic rose, and generally a better rose than Golden Showers but the trouble is for those who want a really golden yellow this rose won't quite make the mark. The flowers are a softer blowsier yellow though they do have a lovely form and scent. **The Pilgrim** is another excellent yellow rose, perhaps more citrus in colour under direct sunlight. It is a very good rose to grow above a front door.

Pink and beyond

Albertine has a romantic, practical and pleasingly old-fashioned feel. If I could have only one rose against the side of my house it would be this one. Mine tolerates a north-easterly corner of the house and spends much of the year festooned with large pinky, coppery flowers that look well in a vase on your desk. It will romp away happily, reaching the roof of a two-storey house with ease. **New Dawn** is a brighter pink by contrast whose smallish flowers are full of romantic charm. It was developed in the 1930s and it was my wife's grandmother's favourite rose. I adored my wife's grandmother and she had a quiet and entirely un-pompous love of plants. I had a beautiful New Dawn in my last garden which was really thriving until the neighbours took down the wall it had been growing against! Foolishly I have not planted one in this garden yet. This is a very pleasing and classic rose that will make ten to twelve feet in height comfortably.

Roses for real altitude

Paul's Himalayan Musk is a very good candidate for a tree. It has clusters of smaller pink to white flowers that look like sea spray as they climb through a host's boughs. This rose is a rambler not a climber and will travel perhaps as high as thirty feet or more given time; but being a rambler don't expect season round flowers. **Rambling Rector** would be an alternative with even more verve and vigour. It is certainly the rose of choice if you want to completely smother an ungainly outbuilding. However, whilst it has healthy and attractive foliage, being a rambler it will flower once only in June, though these are lovely pure white. Its hips and foliage will go a long way towards compensating for a single flowering. **Kiftsgate** is another famously rumbustious rambler that will make fifty feet or more and throw out a strong fragrance. Not a rose to plant in an ordinary flowerbed.

– Roses for the border –

Roses often look best when planted in company. Roses can develop quite bare legs and of course this can be greatly mitigated in the context of a mixed border, but equally I don't think any other plant is quite so good at breaking up a border or creating punctuation within it.

Roses are expensive but they are also among the easiest plants to propagate. A little trip to a friend or relative's garden in early September with a pair of secateurs and a pot containing compost laced with horticultural grit should be seriously considered. Cut just below a bud to remove a section a foot or so long and at least as thick as a pencil. Remove all but a few leaves and slide the cutting two thirds down between the side of the pot and the compost (keeping it the right way up as you go). When you get home place it in a sheltered spot outside and water. There is a very high chance that the following season you will have a rose to plant out.

White

As with climbing roses finding a really good white rose for the border can, surprisingly, be something of a challenge. **Silver Anniversary** is a strong contender with very decent looking flowers (like the ones florists like to use) which makes it good for cutting for the house, but the overall plant is a bit small, so it wants to be towards the front of a border. David Austin has **Winchester Cathedral** and also **Desdemona,** both of which are larger and more likely to hold their own in a mixed border and have fuller heads.

Red

Darcey Bussell is my absolute go-to recommendation for a good red rose. I like **Thomas à Becket** too but it throws off quite an arresting shade of red. I want to give a rose with a very dark red colour called **Deep Secret** a chance in this garden but haven't yet found the place to put it.

Yellow

Peace provides yellow with a twist, which is an edging of pink to the petals! This is an absolute classic hybrid tea rose and has that classic rose look. It was introduced in 1945 and quickly became one of the most popular roses in the world. It will hold its own in any mixed border or rose garden. However, if you want that thick proper yellow, like molten gold, then try **Arthur Bell**: it has won plenty of awards and my ones have proved to be pretty disease free, with a nice shape and lusty green foliage.

Pink and beyond

I love the **Queen of Sweden,** I really do. Whilst the appealing soft pink colour and scent are both perfectly good I like it for the unusual form of its flowers. They open into polite little cups that never seem to lose themselves in spilling over. If you had one before you, this would make complete sense. And they grow into a splendid confident shape. This is a very good rose for a border and will make a decent height too. **Boscobel** is another excellent David Austin rose that will hold itself well in a mixed border and has a wonderful coppery pink flower and brilliant scent. I couldn't recommend these two roses more highly and they work well together too. I helped name **The Modern Slavery Rose** as part of my work for the Modern Slavery Garden that went to the Chelsea Flower Show in 2016. Despite this cause for bias, it has become, without any exaggeration, one of my all-time favourite roses. Its buds are flecked with hot scarlet streaks and open into a colour that is quite a long way towards true apricot (something of a rarity in rose breeding). The flowers fade elegantly, furnishing an unusually graceful demise. I have found mine grow healthy and the shape develops with a mixture of politeness but also surprising deftness. Sadly I have no financial links with the excellent Northern Irish rose nursery that bred it!

Wild roses

Rosa Rugosa is a species or 'wild' rose and as a result it is very healthy and disease free, though tracing its pedigree from Asia it will also flower through the season. It has a further advantage in being incredibly tough and capable of thriving in almost any conditions you can throw at it. You can get it in both white and pink and all of them have generous hips the size of small apples that have the power to hugely enhance an autumn stroll. Its only drawback is unusually menacing spikes.

People usually think of *Rosa rugosa* for a hedge but I see no reason not to plant them in a stand-alone capacity towards the back of a border and in fact because they are generally thought of for a hedge it is easy to buy them during the winter as hedging whips (as opposed to plants in pots) and in this guise they are likely to cost no more than a couple of pence. For all these reasons I think they are a good choice particularly if you are building a garden on a budget. **Rosa Moyesii** is another species rose with wonderfully shaped hips well worth considering, though it will flower only once.

– *Clematis, honeysuckle and lavender* –

If roses are the most popular English garden plant (and I believe they probably are) there must be some sort of competition between clematis and lavender for the position of second place. There are now a huge number of clematis varieties on offer, some, like the ubiquitous Montana, flower early and are useful if you want to smother an unsightly outbuilding; others will climb to no more than a few feet. But what many people don't realise is that it is possible to have one type of clematis or another flowering pretty much all through the year, and in fact the winter-flowering cirrhosa varieties are among my very favourite.

How to prune a clematis (which is definitely an area of possible confusion for anyone starting out with them) is in fact based on when they flower. Pruning group one is for those that flower in mid spring, pruning group two covers those that flower in May and June and pruning group three covers those that flower later in the summer. Group one should be pruned immediately after flowering, group two can be given a light prune after flowering, with a sterner one the following February and those in group three are pruned in February.

If all this sounds confusing it is perfectly okay to simply say to yourself that those in group one can get chopped back when they start growing where you don't want them and all the others can be chopped back to within a foot of the ground and mulched in February either every year, or otherwise every few years. That is what I do and it works for me.

There are certain tips that apply to all clematis regardless of when they flower. The first is to ensure that when you plant them you bury their stems a little deeper in the ground (a few inches, anyway) than they were growing in the pot. This helps ward off a disease clematis are particularly prone to. Secondly, it is never a bad idea to provide a little shade at their base, even by placing a few larger stones around them. Finally, regardless of which pruning group they are in, all clematis ideally want a strong prune to a foot or so above the ground in their first spring after planting.

Honeysuckle is another useful clambering plant. Japanese honeysuckle is very useful because it is semi evergreen, though my ones keep their leaves all winter and they will climb very high, even to thirty feet or more. They also have a nice long flowering period through to the end of summer. For both these reasons I think it is a nice plant to have near to a house. The scarlet trumpet honeysuckle is worth looking at too for its interesting leaves and red berries. It is listed as a semi-evergreen but mine always seems to keep its leaves. Late Dutch honeysuckle is the classic and smells fabulous but is deciduous and as the name suggests, late flowering. For earlier flowering choose Early Dutch. Honeysuckles can be usefully grown into a tree though clearly they won't achieve the same height as a boisterous rambling rose.

In France lavender grows (like the other Mediterranean herbs) in crags and crannies on dry mountainsides. As a result if you grow it here you want to ensure excellent drainage, even going so far as planting it into a gathered up mound (of course, with horticultural grit added). If you want your lavender to keep a tight shape you will also have to prune it probably twice a year, at the beginning and end of the growing season. Even if you do this it will need replacing frequently, perhaps even every five years. In the wild, lavender plants might live for ten or fifteen years during which period they will become leggy and ancient looking. As it happens I rather like this look and I grow my lavender as a backing to the sweet pea border precisely so I don't have to keep it looking too sharp. Mine gets a quick haircut just after growth starts and shows plenty of ancient leg!

My lavender never suffers from pests or disease but I imagine it might do so more in the wetter parts of the country, particularly if it is being pruned hard to keep it tight and therefore being encouraged to make plenty of sappy growth. My father had great beds of lavender directly adjacent to the windows of our house in order that its scent would waft in on a hot summer's breeze. It is perfectly sensible to harvest your lavender and dry it in order to scent your wardrobes and of course the right varieties offer culinary uses that are rarely exploited. I remember as a boy making lavender bread, and the look on my father's face as he nibbled politely away at a corner of it.

Lavender self-seeds quite strongly, particularly in gravel. When it does this I generally let the plants develop. When I was growing up, I remember people always saying that lavender liked a scattering of blood and bone in the spring but these days I don't tend to feed my lavender at all and have so far noticed no disadvantage, perhaps the opposite. You have to treat Mediterranean herbs rough; coddle them and pay the price.

– Coping with difficult spots –

Most gardens have their difficult spots. You may have a patch of soil that is waterlogged and boggy, into which you will have to place plants that can cope with extreme damp. Alternatively, your issue might be quite the opposite, you might have a sunny patch of sharp draining soil at a distance from the house that you simply can't be bothered to water but you still want to look nice. Some corners of the garden might be particularly shaded, or worst of all you might have a combination of dry and shade known as 'dry shade'. If this is caused by a nearby evergreen tree, and if that tree happens to be a leylandii, this effect can be very great indeed. It should be stated clearly that some battles with 'dry shade' are not worth fighting!

The first step is making an assessment about what conditions the various parts of your garden provide. How much light reaches a certain spot is relatively easy to discern by visiting it at various times of the day and considering how much of the day it might spend in direct sunlight, particularly in the summer. But when considering how much water a particular spot might get it is worth thinking about rain shadows.

It is obvious, for example, that a tree will direct rain to the edge of its canopy and as a result the soil around its trunk will be both dry and shaded. But people don't always consider that if your weather is predominantly south-westerly (as it is in Britain) it stands to reason that a tree will cast a rain shadow to its north-east that stretches beyond its canopy. The same is true of walls, fences and houses.

To compound matters, people also often don't consider that walls themselves are like giant sponges and the soil immediately adjacent to them is therefore almost always dry. This in itself is a good reason to never plant directly against a wall but rather at least a foot or so from it. Climbing plants, for example, should then be directed back onto the wall from a slight distance. And remember a patch of soil to the north-east of a wall might be very dry indeed.

But all gardens are different. For example, I garden in Essex which is a dry county and yet I have a friend a few miles away whose soil is always gorgeously irrigated and whose lawns, when all of ours are parched and yellow, are green and springy underfoot. This is not because he waters them, it is because his whole property sits on a series of springs, so you do have to get to know your individual garden.

Whilst the soil under a large tree will be drier and more shaded than other parts of your garden this doesn't mean that it can't be enlivened. If the tree is deciduous, the most obvious way to pick up such an area is to use spring bulbs. Spring bulbs have evolved precisely to do their photosynthesising in the spring before leaf break so this is their way of surviving life under a tree. I have found yellow aconites are the most shade tolerant of the lot.

It is instructive to look at this whole area from the perspective of nature itself. A short walk through woodland will illustrate how a number of ferns, or for that matter ivy, are often quite happy in considerable shade. Actually, not only is ivy in my opinion very attractive, but because it flowers in the winter it is an absolute lifeline for insects. Another similar plant is what used to be called periwinkle, usually marketed as Vinca, and there are not many areas where vinca or ivy won't grow. Again, a short walk through a forest will show that brambles can be quite shade tolerant and you may not know that there are some particularly attractive brambles, including the ghost white wands of the ludicrously named *Rubus cockburnianus*. Fundamentally, the thing to do with difficult spots is to try to establish how nature herself solves the same problem.

A few plants commonly considered for very damp soil	Gunnera I Astilbes I Marsh Marigold
A few plants commonly considered for very dry soil	Lavender and the other Mediterranean herbs I Salvias I Cistus I Sea Hollies I Snow in Summer
A few plants commonly considered for shady soil	Ajuga I Anemones I some Ferns I *Alchemilla mollis* I maybe Foxgloves
A few plants commonly considered for dry shade (in circumstances where battle is worth commencing)	Bergenias I Brunnera I Vinca I Ivy I maybe Cyclamen

– *What is a shrub?* –

Technically a shrub is any plant with multiple woody stems. Plants with single woody stems are trees or standards and those with only sappy growth clearly aren't shrubs. That said, the definition is somewhat porous. A rose is technically a shrub but as we have seen a shrub rose is merely a rose that can't be placed into one of the other named categories. At the other end of the spectrum, a small tree might be a shrub. For example, is a multi-stemmed hazel growing on the edge of a wood a shrub or a tree? In a sense, who cares. And yet, we all know what we mean by a shrub and we don't really mean multi-stemmed hazels growing on the edge of woods, we mean plants, sometimes evergreen, that grow relatively large on many stems and add volume and pace to a border.

The Victorians were keen on dedicated shrubberies. Whilst many people do not have the room for a dedicated shrubbery, I think it is a shame to discount the concept from horticulture entirely. I have one and I am very grateful for the good offices of the previous owner, without whom I would not have one. You need a bit of patience to establish a shrubbery: at least five years. Mine was probably started twenty years ago and sits behind the path that runs along the back of the snaking sweet pea border. As such it both shields and frames the sweet pea bed and because it is evergreen it does so throughout the year. It also provides real vertical drama in the garden.

Shrubs are generally bought small but grow large so one of the most common errors when people lay out a shrubbery is to plant the specimens too close together. This is very easy to do because the plant that you put in the ground looks nothing like the one that will be before you in five years' time and that one in turn often looks nothing like the plant that you hope will flourish in fifteen years' time. Planting a shrubbery requires discipline and you must either plant with large gaps and resign yourself to the whole thing looking naked for a few years or, I suppose, you could over-plant and resign yourself to some sort of future 'thinning out'.

The other thing to consider is that you need to stagger shrubs in a shrubbery. There is no point planting a low-growing shrub like hebe in the middle of a large patch of photinia because it will never amount to much and may eventually succumb to the evergreen canopy above it. Hebe, as it happens, is a very good shrub for the front of a shrubbery. It remains the case, however, that you are more likely to find shrubs these days being used to break up a border. What follows are five of my favourites.

– *Five good flowering shrubs* –

Mock orange

Also known commonly as Philadelphus, these deciduous shrubs were among my father's favourites for the sweet citrus perfume of their flowers. If allowed to it will grow quite large so probably best for the back of a border though this is a definite advantage because it will produce more and larger stems for cutting and bringing inside. Great boughs can be placed in vases and will fill even the largest room with a sweet summer scent. This works famously in bathrooms because the steam from a hot bath seems to lift and carry the scent further still.

Flowering currants

I like one called King Edward VII for its garish red flowers in spring. These flowers sit above the deciduous foliage which is both neat and of the crispest green, making for a quite dramatic display. The shrub can be kept relatively tidy so could accordingly creep forward in a border. If you want to give it a trim do so after flowering. You will notice the flowers don't smell, but the foliage does.

Daphne

These are undoubtedly among the most beautifully scented plants on planet earth and their delicate fragrance, which often comes early in the year, when winter is still fresh in the memory, has a haunting beauty. I think they work well near to the front door of a house for this reason. There are both deciduous and evergreen varieties. As you know already they don't like being moved and because they tend to be slow growing and hard to propagate they are also quite expensive. You have been warned.

Buddleia

Common and as tough as old boots but with a beautiful and I think well-scented flower. Also known as the butterfly bush. Buddleia that are allowed to romp can often get leggy (with their flowers held miles in the air and their legs exposed immodestly) but this is easy to remedy as their inherent robustness means they think little of even pretty violent pruning. New lower growing dwarf varieties are also now available which might be a better bet for the front of a border.

There are soft golden yellows to add to the more commonly seen rich purples, blues and whites. Buddleia are among the easiest plants to propagate, so they are a good candidate if you are starting a garden on a limited budget. Whilst deciduous they can make an attractive summer hedge if cut to the right point each spring.

Mahonia

If you think about it, so many of the earliest flowers are yellow: daffodils, primrose, forsythia, laburnum, even yellow

113

roses tend to come before the others, but the astonishingly scented yellow flowers that droop generously on racemes in late winter from the Mahonia are among the very best. The shrub is also evergreen giving it year-round presence in the border.

Mahonia prefers a reasonably sheltered spot and isn't troubled by a little shade. If you want an evergreen flowering shrub for a sunnier aspect try Californian Lilac, which is a supremely useful garden plant and flowers with the most delicate blue throughout the summer. I grow a variety called Puget Blue that is said to be well suited to clay soil but I have grown others and all that I have tried have been good. In my experience Californian Lilacs don't enjoy pruning, so best to keep it to a minimum.

– *Taking cuttings and layering* –

O ne of the miraculous things about plants is that very often you can make more of them by fooling a section of tissue that wouldn't ordinarily form roots to do just that. This is called taking a cutting. Sometimes it is worth taking a cutting simply because lots of plants can be made quickly and cheaply when compared to either growing from seed or buying them in (as with lavender and box). At other times, with plants that don't come true from seed, you might take a cutting to preserve the particular quality of the parent. But in general cuttings are a gardener's natural 'hack' for arriving at more plants.

When you start a cutting (take a segment of plant material and place it into a pot or nursery bed hoping it will grow into a new plant) a race begins; can the plant produce sufficient roots to support the growth of new foliage before it withers above or rots below? This is because the cutting will need to retain enough foliage above ground to keep photosynthesising but not so much that it is spending moisture it can't replace from the developing root system. As soon as the cutting starts to grow away strongly you can say it has 'struck'. Sometimes it fools you and grows some foliage only to wilt back and die because it was unsuccessful (or rotted off) at the other end.

Even for the most experienced gardener, taking a cutting is always a gamble but there are various general rules you can follow which will improve your chances:

- Spray water into a sealable plastic bag with your atomiser and when you walk around a garden taking sappy green cuttings place them immediately into this plastic bag and seal it so that the plant material remains as hydrated as possible. Get the cuttings into pots as soon as possible, don't stop for a chat.
- Take your cuttings in the morning when plant material is most turgid (full of water) before the day's sunshine bleeds it of moisture.
- When you take the cutting from the plant cut the lower section flat across and the higher section at a slant so you remember which way is up. This is also useful if you are running several cuttings off a single stem.
- Always try to take a cutting from a non-flowering stem if possible.
- Use a sharp knife so you don't tear sappy material.
- Always use a soil or compost mix with plenty of horticultural grit added to improve drainage and decrease the chance of roots rotting.
- Using a pencil for a dibber push the plant material between the edge of the pot and the compost because this seems to help prevent rotting and increase the chance of a cutting striking.
- Try to balance the amount of foliage on your cutting to just enough but not too much. This really is a question of judgment and practice but be assured if you have a cutting with a single large leaf, taking the radical step of cutting this leaf back by a half or two thirds might be perfectly reasonable.
- Once the cuttings are in their pots mist them regularly with an atomiser as this can help keep the top growth hydrated. However, after initially watering the cuttings

be wary of watering too much because this may encourage rot.

- Cuttings want light but certainly not the withering effects of direct sunlight, which in their rootless state can wilt them rapidly.

Cuttings are broken down in gardening books into hardwood, softwood and semi-ripe cuttings. I have always considered these distinctions to be potentially confusing to the newcomer, which is why I have left them to the end of the section.

Traditionally hardwood cuttings (buddleia, roses or for that matter mock orange or flowering currant) were taken in the autumn and placed directly into nursery beds outside. I have found the best moment is often just before their buds break in the spring, but in either case the cuttings are taken when the plant is essentially dormant.

Softwood cuttings (pelargoniums, hydrangeas or for that matter petunias) are taken in late spring and early summer when the green sappy material is growing. Semi-ripe cuttings (good for box, lavender or rosemary) are so called because the material taken is soft and sappy at the growing end, though starting to harden at the base. As such they are only available in late summer or early autumn.

These distinctions are useful for planning when to take any given cutting, but I have found it useful also to hold on to the simplifying thought that whenever you take a cutting, you are asking a plant to do the same thing: break roots where previously it wouldn't have.

If you want to start taking cuttings I would advise you to start out at the easier end (buddleia, lavender, box, pelargonium, rose). In fact, when you next prune your buddleia in early spring, if you simply cut a foot or two from below a bud and plunge it into the ground, making sure two thirds of its length goes below the surface of the soil, most of the time it will strike and if it doesn't it is probably because it got nibbled or stepped on. As mentioned, this makes buddleia a great plant if you're starting a garden on a budget.

– *Concluding Part III* –

Now you are not only encouraging plants to put down their roots in your garden but you are also putting your own roots down quite deep into the soil of British horticulture. Deeper than you think! You are familiar with eighty of the most common garden plants, you understand how it is that we have got to the point where we have such a large selection of roses to grow and you are equipped to take on tricky spots. You will also no doubt be thinking about making sure that something is not just happening in your garden in each of the four seasons but happening well. Remember 'well' just means to your taste, it matters not a jot what someone down the road might think about your choices.

You will do things that you later consider to be 'mistakes'. I suspect, however hard you try, you will find that you have planted some things, inside and outside the vegetable garden, too closely together. The urge in the heart of the new gardener not to have too much in the way of large gaps is absolutely automatic and pushing up against that urge really is one of the things that has to be learnt. I suspect you will have planted something and then changed your mind about where it should be. You may well have moved it successfully, but if you are anything like me there will have been a few casualties along the way too.

Very soon (if not already) you will start to see these 'mistakes' as just the corollary of working with nature and striving to partner it better each season. Last year I lost almost my entire crop of peas to slugs. Perhaps I should have waited until the plants were bigger before setting them out. Two years previously I lost almost my entire crop of peas to mice breaking into the cold frames and eating them under my nose. In the intervening year I had a massive, resplendent crop of peas. The whole family gathered round the pea sticks and snacked on them direct from the pods in all their freshly picked pea-ness. As you grow peas you will pick up different things about them. They don't like mice or slugs but neither do they like really hot weather.

You will also, I hope, have sallied forth with a sharp knife and a plastic bag intent on making more plants from your existing stock. Some will wilt. Some will strike. This is gardening; learning to accept the lost and gained harvest. Thinking and, just as importantly, feeling your way into a better and better stewardship of nature. Facts are important, but gardening is an art before it is a science.

Part IV

We must have vegetables

– Enjoying the fat of the land –

Despite having enough space to feed a small hamlet or run a vegetable box scheme I don't see the point of trying to be self-sufficient. My garden simply isn't a small farm. During a war there are perfectly sound reasons for straining towards self-sufficiency, but to my mind it is a matter of regret that this attitude has rather set the tone for vegetable growing ever since the last one. And the whole sorry concept was given a boost in the 1970s by the television programme *The Good Life*, whose effects seem to linger to this day.

The reason I resent this approach is because it seems to turn the whole act of growing vegetables into guilt-driven labour, when really it should be a matter of supreme joy. Eating is one of life's great pleasures and the quality and variety of the seasonal produce in our local supermarkets and smaller food shops (especially our farm shops) is excellent. Besides, I like popping into shops. For me vegetable growing isn't about self-sufficiency; it is about eating not just well, but supremely well. I think people respond to luxury with more enthusiasm than they do to grunt.

For me, the vegetable patch shouldn't simply supplement what is bought at the till, it should augment it. It isn't about the means of production but about utter delectability. With this in mind I try to think about the whole thing more like a chef and less like a gardener. Each year I think not about what I might like to grow, but what I might like to eat. It is much more fun that way.

What does this mean? One year I seriously considered slaving the entire vegetable patch to delivering foods and flavours I remembered from my childhood. There would be nothing wrong with growing bay leaves simply to make the perfect omelette Arnold Bennett, or caraway seeds for a cake or marrow for marrow and ginger jam, so why not carry this approach to its logical conclusion. Better to grow for a menu than from a catalogue.

In the normal run of things I keep a supply of squashes coming into the kitchen all summer because I can't find the ones I like if I don't grow them and I love nothing more than baking a squash stuffed with cheese, meat, herbs or all three. I like white currants and they're hard to find in shops. I grow big beds of basil because I can never buy enough in the supermarket, and that is true of all herbs. Take five or six good handfuls of basil from the garden, chop it into a big bowl and add warm tomatoes fresh from the vine and you will know what I mean. Incidentally, chilling kills the flavour of a tomato, which is another good reason to grow your own.

I grow Anya potatoes as an early crop simply because they are the best and you can't guarantee finding them in the shops and a season without them would be a waste of a year. I grow Pink Fir Apple potatoes as a main crop for the same reason. As you already know I grow strawberries and particularly wild strawberries because you can never get the latter in the shops either.

What I am about to write may provoke howls of derision but to my mind gardening and vegetable growing are actually quite different activities. Here is the test. I grow some vegetables in my garden. The large fleshy green leaves of rhubarb look well in a border and it causes quite a stir when it flowers.

Artichokes I grow for their flowers, to be sure. I grow red kale just because it looks nice. These plants are not for eating and I think entirely differently about them; they are not bound by the ultimate goal of ending up on a chopping board. They play their part in a different poem. The poetry of the vegetable garden takes place on the kitchen table and the vegetable garden itself often looks fairly dreadful.

Getting a vegetable garden to look good for a photographer from a magazine or newspaper is far more worrisome than the garden itself. The vegetable patch is a place where you should unleash your inner chef first and your inner gardener only in a supporting role. It is about eating not looking, and that is why it is always sensible to shield a veg patch with a wall or hedge!

I like chickens well enough and I keep them, but I do it ultimately because I am after their eggs. I keep dogs too, but I would never eat them. They fall into different camps. If I could I would have a tethered Jersey cow and make my own butter and I would add much more salt than the shop bought stuff has; and it would be excellent Maldon salt and I would use too much of it. You get the point. My veg patch is about eating, not gardening. As with Churchill's comments about alcohol, I make sure I get a lot more out of it than it gets out of me!

– *Where to position the vegetable patch* –

This is a critical question and, sadly, is usually answered incorrectly. It is a shame because in a larger garden the simple choice over where to site your veg patch will almost certainly be the determining factor in how much you enjoy it, possibly over a lifetime. Unfortunately many of my friends who have started on new garden adventures not only answer the question incorrectly, they seem to do so boldly. Though of course they don't see it that way at the time. For historical reasons there is a general sense that the vegetable patch should be somewhere vaguely 'off'. Wrong.

Unless you have an army of gardeners there is only one place for a vegetable patch to be: as close to the kitchen door as possible. Any romantic ideas based on a Wodehousian sense of the proper order of things are out of date. For the vast bulk of us the correct place for a vegetable patch is the spot with enough light and enough shelter that is closest to the external door of the house that is itself closest to the kitchen. That is all there is to it.

– Crop rotation –

As a general rule growing the same crop in the same position year in year out is a bad idea. Plants have a complex relationship with the soil and take a range of different minerals and substances from it. Certain plants take more of one thing than of another and so repeated cropping of the same species will leave the soil increasingly depleted of a certain suite of minerals. Worse still, some plants are vulnerable to soil-borne diseases so repeated production will build up a reservoir of disease in the earth. In essence soil needs to be allowed to 'rest' so it can restock on nutrients and be cleansed of any disease or blight. In a vegetable patch this means rotating the crops you grow.

There are five basic groups of vegetables:

Solanaceae – potatoes, tomatoes etc

Roots – carrot, beetroot etc

Legumes – peas, broad beans etc

Onions – chives, leek etc

Brassicas – sprouts, cauliflower etc

People get complicated and propose ideal rotations, so that, for example, brassicas follow legumes to take advantage of the nitrogen the legumes have fixed in the soil but my advice is not to go into too much detail. Just make sure you rotate these families a bit. We all forget from time to time but the ones to watch chiefly are potatoes and tomatoes because they both suffer from the same blight so treat them as the same crop and switch their growing position every year.

– Getting a vegetable bed ready –

Traditionally vegetable beds were loaded with muck in the autumn and left over winter so that by the time of spring sowing you had lovely refreshed soil. The sight of rows of vegetable beds in the autumn smothered with a thick greedy layer of muck, like toast teetering with an impolite layer of jam, is the sort of sight that gets gardeners very excited.

One advantage of doing this in the autumn is that no digging is required. Between the effect of frost (which helps break clumps up) and worms (which drag the nutrients deep into the soil) little effort is required on the part of the gardener. Worms go deeper into the soil when it gets very cold so a slathering in early autumn (rather than midwinter) is best.

People sometimes ask me if they can add muck at this or that time of the year. The answer has two parts. The only thing you need watch with muck is that it has rotted down sufficiently so that the urea doesn't burn plants. This is less of a consideration if you don't intend to plant into the bed in question any time soon. The second part of the answer is that as with any mulching, you can do it whenever you wish so long as you aren't mulching over a dry soil because mulch will lock moisture in but also out.

Not all vegetables want a rich soil. I have found that onions grown in too rich a soil sometimes grow extravagant foliage on a little bulb (which matters, because the bulb can be largely pointless) and carrots will fork out in a million odd directions (which doesn't really matter, they just look odd). So some forward planning is required when you feed your beds in autumn.

When it comes to preparing a bed for the first time I have come to increasingly reject the traditional approach to digging. I am not quite evangelical about 'no dig' but I am something of a reformed digger. When I started out I threw myself into digging with great gusto. I was all for intervention and I followed what I read in the books, and my books are fairly traditional so I did a large amount of digging. Digging goodness into the soil, regular digging to break soil up, double digging to start a new bed; if in doubt just dig and then dig a little more.

Double digging involves digging two spits (two lengths of a spade) deep. Conventional wisdom dictates that this very labour-intense system is the best way to charge the soil with nutrients prior to growing vegetables or starting a herbaceous border. But each time you put steel in the soil, be it a plough or a spade, you are altering a pre-existing and delicate system within it (microbes, fungi and the like) and this is likely to degrade it rather than enhance it. I would go so far as to say that I am now irritated with myself for all the double digging I did when I started this garden, but there it is.

Increasingly I make it my business not to interfere with natural processes if I don't have to. In nature there is an awful lot of mulching, every autumn during leaf fall and throughout the year via animal droppings, it just happens extremely slowly. This is in fact how soil is made, but measured in millimetres per century, which is why soil erosion is such a concern. On the other hand, disregarding a little poaching from animal hooves and the odd badgers' set, very little digging happens in nature. Digging (which on a large scale is called ploughing) is hominoid. In nature large pieces of metal just don't get dragged through soil. You can make a new bed by digging it, or you can make a new bed by mulching it heavily and now I choose mulching as far as is practical.

There is a mass of literature out there on both no till farming and no dig gardening, and going into the details of how digging might influence life below the soil in any detail is beyond the scope of this book but I, for one, am now convinced. To my shame it was not until I discussed the matter in detail with a local farming friend who had gone no till that I became convinced; it just makes a huge amount of sense.

I have had plenty of success simply scalping grass with the mower, using scaffolding boards to enclose an area with a layer of cardboard or a few sheets of newspaper under a good foot and a half of mulch. I have found this works perfectly well and restricts the grass and weeds below adequately, provided it is accompanied with some routine follow up weeding. More recently I have dispensed with the newspaper and instead invert the contents of the compost heap, placing the green under-composted material over the scalped grass first (which acts like a newspaper barrier) and the good well-composted material on top. I have large compost heaps and achieve a good foot and a half of mulch over the new beds, and so far it is working well. Squashes are a good first crop for such an arrangement.

Recently I started a new bed on grass but scaffolding boards weren't appropriate so I cut turves and simply turned them over and put them back into the hole from which they had come. If you had only a thin layer of topsoil this strategy wouldn't work, but in this particular spot I have a good eight inches of topsoil so the inverted turf presented usable soil and I could get away with it. I gave the whole area a good foot of mulch. This is not strict 'no dig' but it's certainly 'less dig' than I have been used to. It worked well.

– *Composting basics* –

Leaves and twigs represent 'brown' carbon rich material and grass and animal wallop represent 'green' nitrogen rich material. The secret to composting is to get the balance of these two materials right. Too much brown and the heap won't do enough actual rotting, too much green (for example grass cuttings in the summer) and you might end up with slurry. Some people add brown and green in layers, but I just keep an eye on the heap to make sure it is being fed with sufficient variety. Fed is the right word, because hungry bacteria are turning your garden waste into black gold.

Animal wallop from horses, cows or birds is all particularly good to add though bird wallop (guano) has the highest nutrient content. On the other hand I fancy that horse wallop is the most efficient at conditioning the soil and cow muck is the best for roses. There is no science in that view, just my opinion. Whatever you do don't add dog, cat, fox or badger poo.

Keeping chickens is of course a good way to feed a composting system and a number of firms now provide chicken coops with the city garden in mind. For most people who live in the country it isn't too hard to find a local stables or farmer who is willing to help you out.

Cooking good quality nutrient rich compost holds all the pleasure of the *Bake Off* stretched over about six months, and the first time you add a shovel full of your own home-made compost to the garden is a stand out moment in the life of any gardener.

Speeding things up

Unless you are a very patient person, I guarantee when you start your first heap you will be impatient to get to the end of the process as quickly as possible. Here are four things to keep in mind if you wish to speed things up:

- Make sure when you add material it is in the smallest size possible. Leaves can be mown over, paper can be torn and woody material can be shredded or more simply snapped.
- Add an activator. Pee is the best but seaweed meal will do if you are squeamish.
- Boost the work of the bacteria by adding more oxygen. This can be achieved by turning the heap with a fork or even prodding it with a stick.
- Don't let the heap dry out. It is a good idea to dowse a compost heap with water before working it anyway because this keeps little fungal spores down that can be a health risk for some people.

If you do none of these things you will, of course, still get compost though it might just take longer.

Warding off unwanted visitors

The single biggest challenge when managing a compost heap is, of course, warding off rats. From their perspective the heap is a warm five-star hotel. However, rats are phobic of change

134

so oftentimes simply turning the heap is enough to dispense with them. On the other hand, once they have identified a good source of food, so long as nothing changes, they will keep coming back to it with determined regularity. This is useful knowledge if you are a good shot and know how to use an air rifle safely. I consider this method, or the good offices of a terrier, far more humane and environmentally friendly than the use of poison, which slowly dissolves the rats' internal organs.

What can go on?

The Japanese have a special composting system for meat called Bokashi but if you don't run a Bokashi system don't add meat! In fact, I never add anything that has been cooked or processed in any way at all so this includes bread, breakfast cereal and even supposedly innocuous cooked vegetables because having been cooked they are easy to digest and rats love them. There are items that sit on a borderline. Egg shells are rather good for the compost heap itself, but rats seem marginally attracted to them, so I add them when I don't have a rat problem and not when I do.

I don't add anything tainted by oil, grease or dairy fat because it would greatly impede the quality and usefulness of the end product. Plants don't want oily toes. Whereas most kitchen waste is green, most household waste is brown. Add anything that is paper or cardboard but watch for too much ink. The cardboard inners of loo or kitchen rolls are an easy yes, as are cardboard boxes if you shred them into smaller pieces. Newspaper is okay but not too much. Shiny cardboard that has been printed on with garish colours is no good and glossy magazines are a disaster. Wood ash is good but not too much.

Yes	No
Coffee grounds and tea leaves or plastic-free tea bags	Cereal scraps or bread
Vegetable and fruit peelings (watch too much citrus)	Meat, milk or dairy
Rejected parts of vegetables	Cooked vegetables or anything that has touched oil
Wood ash (not too much)	Animal excrement
Loo roll and kitchen roll inners, newspaper (not too much)	Heavily inked cardboard or glossy magazine paper
Grass cuttings, leaves and small prunings	Sticks or larger woody material (unless chipped)
Old houseplants, old compost etc	Nasty perennial weeds (bindweed, couch grass etc)

– Vegetable groups I wouldn't be without –

In a previous section I have detailed how I deal with tomatoes, squashes and lettuce, so here are a few additional
vegetable groups I wouldn't be without.

Potatoes

Potatoes are fun. I don't know why that should be but they
are. For a start they are so simple. You put one in and if you
are lucky get ten back. Also, potatoes in the kitchen are so
versatile; they can be boiled, mashed, chipped or preferably
roasted. They can be used to top pies, beef up stews or, in
one of their various guises, accompany pretty much any
other food. We get very excited when the first crop of waxy
salad potatoes rolls in and, like most people, we eat them
lightly boiled with lots of butter and freshly chopped garden
mint. But we also find that you can lift a mash with a drizzle of truffle oil and chips with a humous dip is a fine
Sunday evening dinner. In my lexicon chips should be salted
and then slathered with masses of Bristol five blend pepper
before being subjected to a dressing of grated parmesan
cheese.

When it comes to growing potatoes there are a few pieces
of gardening lingo that need to be got through. You will hear
gardeners talking about 'chitting' potatoes. All this means is

leaving them in a bright dry environment (for example a windowsill) for a few weeks before planting in order that they develop a few growing points or 'eyes'. These growing points emerge from the potato and look like little potato arms. There is a general consensus that potatoes should be planted with these little stems sprouting if you want the biggest harvest. You don't have to though. A potato placed in the ground without having been 'chitted' will still provide a harvest.

If you do chit your potatoes the more little stems you leave on the tuber when you put it in the ground the more individual potatoes you are likely to get, but each one will be smaller. Chitting is helpful as a concept because it reveals the fact that there is a compromise to be made when growing potatoes: between lots of small potatoes and a few larger ones. This is clearly a matter of personal preference but most gardeners let their potatoes chit and then rub off all but two or three of the best eyes before planting. Plant so that the eyes are pointing up.

What we call a potato is actually a reserve of energy that enables the plant to break eyes and start its progress from soil to sky. Some gardeners used to cut their tubers in half to make them go further. Whilst this practice no longer seems to carry a consensus of opinion (most people agree seed potatoes should be planted whole) the old method would of course deliver a greater number of potatoes though they would likely be smaller. I find in my own garden new potato plants coming from the smallest scraps that were splintered off during lifting the previous season.

Over time gardeners have tried to develop varieties for harvesting at different times in order to extend the potato season. I wouldn't advise getting too caught up on this; all potatoes will deliver a crop somewhere north of ten weeks after they are planted. Potato planting broadly speaking starts at some point in March and runs until the end of April. If you deploy your potatoes starting with the first earlies and ending with the 'maincrop' varieties you can hope to be harvesting potatoes from June until August. The ground is also a perfectly reasonable place to store a potato (notwithstanding slug attack) so harvesting can carry on well into autumn.

Potatoes are a good crop to break up new ground. If your vegetable patch extends in scope each winter, place your potato crop in the vanguard. If you have limited space you can grow them in a dustbin or even a large bucket so long as it has drainage holes.

I generally dig a trench about four inches deep and just pop them in the ground. First earlies about a ruler's length apart and maincrop potatoes a little over that. I have found the single most important thing with potatoes is to keep them well watered; they don't want to suffer under a punishing sun without water at their feet.

When it comes to choosing which varieties to grow the point of sale material in the plant nursery will leave you in no doubt as to whether a certain variety is considered good for baking, boiling or chipping. Of course, any potato can be subject to the humiliation of any of these forms of execution, but over time you may well find certain varieties work best for you in certain ways. What is indisputable is that there is a marked difference between potatoes that are waxy (generally considered best for light boiling) and those that are fluffy (generally considered best for other uses). I personally consider waxy potatoes to be best for everything: boiling, mashing and chipping. Anya and Pink Fir Apple are both waxy. I do like King Edwards for baking and I find if I rinse them with water and then place them damp into a baking tray with sunflower oil, salt and pepper and give them a really violent thudding shake on the top of the Aga they crisp up beautifully.

Onions and garlic

It is perfectly possible to grow onions each year from seed though most people buy onion 'sets' in the spring from the nursery. An onion set is a small onion that you place in the soil and love and sing to until it becomes a large onion when you eat it. Sounds like a simple process but it attracts more contrary opinion among gardeners than you might imagine.

You might think a nice plump onion set will deliver a nice plump onion but apparently it is now considered better to start with smaller sets. When planted they want to barely touch the soil, and certainly plant no more than a third of their height in depth. Also, whilst you might think that something bold like an onion would want a good nutrient rich soil, they don't. I remember planting sets out one year and congratulating myself on what well fed soil I was planting into. By the end of the season I was presented with thundering great stems and bulbs the same size as when they went in. Growing them in a raised bed is probably best.

Some gardeners start onion sets in modules inside and only set them out once the roots have become established. This has the advantage of ensuring the bulb is planted to just the right depth (because you can back fill compost into the module at the outset) and it gets round the trouble caused by curious blackbirds picking them out of the soil (after which you have to go round pushing them back in again) but it is a greater fiddle, and as you know by now I try to avoid fiddle wherever possible, so I follow the direct approach. My onion sets go out in March. I harvest them when the foliage yellows a little.

I plait them and place them on a metal bench with slats to dry for a few weeks in the sun. Remember red onions tend to be a little sweeter and white ones a little more oniony.

Whilst I love onions, they are no peer for garlic. Unlike onion sets that go out in the spring, the most important thing with garlic is to remember to plant them before Christmas and, frankly, I try to get mine in by the end of September. Garlic wants a good cold winter. My worst garlic harvests have happened when I simply forgot to plant them in time for the best of the cold weather and my best followed the unseasonably cold winter of 2017.

Garlic has much touted antibiotic and antifungal properties and it is commonly considered that land that has grown garlic will provide a benefit to the crop that follows. With absolutely no science but a gardener's nose I try to make garlic the crop that precedes blight prone crops like tomatoes.

For me the whole point of growing garlic is to achieve nice big cloves that are easy to chop and so, in direct contrast to the latest advice on onion sets, you really do want to start big. As you break a bulb up discard all but the biggest cloves with the remainder going to the kitchen or compost heap. Also, because you want nice big cloves at the end of the process it is pointless to overcrowd garlic. If you can't get to the plant nursery it is perfectly sensible to break up a bulb of garlic bought at the supermarket.

If you do go to the plant nursery for your garlic bulbs you will be confronted between a choice of 'hardneck' or 'softneck' varieties. The main difference to grasp is that whilst softneck varieties have smaller bulbs they store better over winter so if you want to eat your own garlic year round it may be sensible to compromise on size. On the other hand hardneck varieties are generally considered to have a stronger flavour which together with their bigger size makes them, to me at least, the more obvious choice.

If a crop of garlic, or more often onion, gets a bad dose of rust there is nothing much you can do about it. If the bulbs are advanced sufficiently the best course is to harvest and eat them. If on the other hand a patch of chives gets a burst of rust, I have chopped them down to soil level and had clean foliage emerge in reward. Rust is encouraged by heat, humidity and a lack of ventilation which is another reason why spacing these crops out (rather than jumbling them together) is preferable.

Beans and peas

There are three types of beans typically grown in English gardens: broad beans, French beans and runner beans. I don't typically grow French beans because they don't like my heavy soil. Of the three, broad beans get the worst press but they are my favourite. Leathery broad beans are disgusting, and even more so if they are overcooked, but this is because people always harvest their broad beans too late. If you harvest them early, when they are still a little soft, delicate and tender, they are delicious and very sweet. You can cook them and add a knob of butter but my favourite method is to eat them straight from the pod.

Broad beans are the easiest of the beans to grow. Some gardeners start them in the autumn for the earliest possible harvest the following spring but the simplest thing is to just sow them where they are to grow when the soil warms in March. I tend to start a crop inside in pots at the end of February, but this is so that when I do plant them out towards the end of March they are large enough to resist the passing attention of slugs. If you want broad beans throughout the summer they can be sown successively until about May.

Some people stake each individual broad bean plant but I consider this an unnecessary faff. The easiest thing is to grow them in blocks of twelve or so plants and then stake the block as a whole with bamboo canes and string. Between the bamboo canes, the string and the various plants knocking into each other this usually keeps them vertical.

One serious potential problem with broad beans is an attack of blackfly that if left will scupper or seriously damage the harvest. The best way to get round this is to pinch out the main growing stem when beans start to form as this restricts the production of further green sappy material which is what the blackfly like. I also find this is a greater problem with later crops.

French beans (or haricot vert) are round and sweet whereas runner beans (or scarlet beans) are flat and long and more fibrous and best chopped into segments before cooking. Whilst broad beans are hardy, both French and runner beans are tender and so should be planted when all risk of frost is past. Both will require a trellis of some sort to scramble up. Both will require consistent watering and the easiest method for both is to sow them directly where they are to grow, in little groups of three, in June.

Runner beans grow large and actually carry very beautiful, often scarlet, flowers. To my mind they could be grown perfectly sensibly for the flowers alone. If you have limited space you could consider growing a pea crop up a support (to be harvested in June) followed by a bean crop (to be harvested at the end of the season).

Broad beans, French beans and runner beans are all good but none quite hits the spot that a beautifully fresh pea can. It is absolutely the case that shop bought peas, even those spot frozen, never taste quite so lovely. Sugars start to denature the moment a vegetable is picked but this is especially noticeable, to my mind, when it comes to peas and carrots.

143

I start a batch of peas inside in pots at the same time as the broad beans and both get planted out by the end of March. I often sow some peas direct when the larger plants go out which starts off the process of successional sowing in one movement. They can then be sown on and off throughout the summer until about May, though they don't like it when it gets too hot.

Spinach (and chard)

Odd it might be but there is almost no vegetable that causes me as much pleasure as spinach. I love being able to amble out and attack the spinach bed for breakfast (fried in a knob of butter with chopped garlic, nutmeg, cinnamon and an egg on top), lunch (to beef up a salad) or dinner (mostly cooked into a curry or spiced with potatoes as a saag aloo).

The seeds are large and can be sown directly into the soil. Start with a seed every inch or two but with spinach it is important that as soon as the seeds germinate you thin them out quite brutally so that each plant has ample room to itself, at least a fully extended hand, as they establish. A second thinning is then advisable, removing every second plant direct to the salad bowl. The plants that are left will grow on to provide a crop of nice large spinach leaves.

The principal danger with spinach is that hot weather will make it bolt and go to seed. As ever, the way to mitigate this danger is to keep it well watered and well picked. It is also sensible to choose varieties that are less likely to bolt and to sow it successionally so that there is always some on the way. Spinach is pretty hardy though it will stop growing in the cold. A patch sown in August will mature by the time of the first frosts and then typically stand all winter. There are green varieties of spinach and there are very attractive red veined varieties. I grow both. There is also something called perpetual spinach (which isn't technically spinach at all) but eats well and will rarely run to seed in its first season, so this is useful if you have dry ground or are limited in your ability to water.

Roots

Personally I like a strong orange colour in my carrots and the sweetest possible flavour. Carrot fly can be a pest but the best advice I have heard is to hold off sowing carrots until early June as this cuts down the chances of developing a problem. As already mentioned, carrots don't want a really rich soil or they will fork and grow in funny shapes, not that this makes them any less edible. If you want long straight carrots don't manure the soil you grow them in the previous autumn.

It stands to reason that carrots will want a reasonable amount of depth in order to grow true (or true to how we like to think of them) so raised beds or even pots make an awful lot of sense. Many vegetables benefit from sowing successionally in order to avoid gluts and this is definitely the way with carrots.

When it comes to sowing carrot seed you can make a little drill and drop them in and then cover them over and water before thinning out when the seedlings emerge. However, carrot seeds are small and fiddly and I have had just as good results through scattering seed willy-nilly on the surface of freshly raked soil and then watering. Before Columbus opened the door to sugar the Elizabethans used carrot as a sweetener and any decent slice of carrot cake is a brave nod to this long forgotten but completely sensible role.

I love beetroot Chioggia (the one with the white and pink stripes through it) for the way it looks, particularly chopped into very fine discs, almost like sashimi, and used to decorate a plate. However, the juicier, meatier, redder varities are better for the baking tray. In fact, the way we most commonly eat beetroot is cut into bleeding red cubes along with squash, carrot and whatever else we can lay our hands on, and baked with a drizzle of olive oil and a few sprigs of rosemary. There is nothing to stop you topping such an arrangement with minced meat or cheese, of course.

Beetroot seeds are very distinct and relatively easy to handle. As a result I tend to make a small drill the depth of my thumb nail and put seeds in every few inches, thinning out as soon as the saplings emerge. Start sowing in March and then keep at it every few weeks for a regular supply through the season. Keep the crop well watered and try to harvest the crop a little early so they don't become too woody. It is as well to remember that the leaves from thinnings can be added to salads too.

Brassicas

The green vegetable that toddlers call trees is in fact more properly called Calabrese. Early purple sprouting broccoli on the other hand is long and thin and has a purple tinge and eaten in season is one of the great culinary delights of the year. The brassica family also includes sprouts, cabbage, cauliflower and the like and they generally sit in the ground for a good while before harvest when compared to other crops.

I do not currently grow all the brassicas every year because whilst I love eating them, especially early purple sprouting broccoli, they impose challenges not common to most other vegetables. They are famously prone to slug, pigeon and whitefly attack so they need careful management but more importantly they require space. My own vegetable patch, having been moved, is currently undergoing a phased enlargement and once this is complete brassica production will commence again in earnest.

Kale is easiest and it is now very popular. The most popular kale to grow is the Italian type, cavolo nero, but I grow kale as much for the way it looks in a flower border as for its taste and as a result I often grow one called Redbor, which, as the name suggests, is a deep purple. I happen to particularly like eating kale but not everyone in this household shares my enthusiasm, so there it is.

It would be well worth growing all the brassicas you can lay your hands on but if you were to choose just two, I would suggest kale and early purple sprouting. Whichever brassicas you choose there are a few universal guidelines. Most brassicas are started inside in modules, or in a nursery bed outside, and then transplanted to the place where they are to grow. To cut down bother many can be bought as small plants from the nursery. Whether you buy in small plants or grow them on yourself, when planting them out into their final positions make sure you firm them in far more strongly than you would for an ordinary plant. It is also a good idea to plant them into a bed that hasn't been dug over for a while because you will never get them in so tight if the soil is light and fluffy.

– *Don't forget perennial vegetables* –

Most people don't consider the fact that certain vegetables are perennials. Think about that! Some of the very best vegetables to eat will, once started, come back year in year out with the minimum of effort. They therefore deliver far more eating bang for far less gardening buck than annuals. We are simply lucky that they are also among the very best the vegetable world has to offer. I have an entire section of my vegetable garden dedicated to perennial vegetables, and this is a course of action I can't recommend highly enough. There are actually far more perennial vegetables than people think, and a little research will pay dividends. Here are three I absolutely wouldn't be without.

Asparagus

Surely the most joyous of the garden vegetable crops. Not only do they mark the arrival of spring proper, but the taste, simply prepared with some butter and salt, is something I spend all year looking forward to. An asparagus bed is an investment in the future. Some time and effort must be put into preparing it properly at the outset but then it will crop for ten or even twenty years, improving as it goes.

Asparagus wants free draining land so if you garden on clay you should improve the drainage with a few bags of horticultural grit and preferably plant into a raised bed. My two asparagus beds are both in raised beds with greatly improved soil. Some varieties of asparagus have long been recommended for heavier soil so it may be worth researching, though I was confident enough with the soil I had prepared to simply choose the varieties I liked the sound of.

The chances are that you will buy your asparagus as two-year-old crowns. These arrive in the post and look like giant spiders. Preferably they will have nice obvious crowns and a profusion of fleshy legs like a giant bare-root strawberry. Just like strawberries these crowns should be soaked for a minimum of an hour in water before planting because the chances are they will have dehydrated in transit. If you delay setting out your plants and allow them to dry entirely you may lose them. That said, I have rehydrated some from what appeared to be a pretty dry state and they grew away fine.

The asparagus crowns will be in situ for many years so you don't want pesky perennial weeds interfering. Either choose a clear spot or give the area a thorough weed at the outset. Once the area is thoroughly weeded clear a trench about three feet wide and a hand deep. Heap the soil (enriched with grit and decent compost) into a mound in the centre of the trench and place the asparagus plants onto the top of the mound, spreading their little legs down into the deeper parts at a distance of at least two feet, in a similar way to making a volcano for strawberry crowns. As with strawberries you want the crowns pretty much at, if not actually over, the soil's surface.

It is important not to pick your asparagus for the first season and preferably for two. Some people say that with certain varieties you can take a Spartan crop; but broadly speaking better to let all the goodness from photosynthesising go back down into the plants' roots to store up proper glory for subsequent years. Even once the plants are established it is strongly advised to stop picking around June so that the late season growth can replenish the goodness in the parts of the plant that are below soil.

The best time to plant the crowns is when the soil warms up so in a challenging March you might wait until April. But I have planted them in a challenging March without too much ill effect, and this can be a lesser risk than the crowns drying out. I water mine in with warm water. If you don't have room for an asparagus bed plop them into a gap in the border. Their lovely feathery foliage will more than pay its way. They will perform in full sun or some shade. Watch planting them in an overly windy location because they are not straightforward to support and growing tall may be vulnerable to wind rock.

Globe artichokes

My mother used to cook me artichokes, before the age when a child might be expected to enjoy them, but I always did. There is something tactile about the process of pulling, dipping and sucking the leaves that I particularly enjoyed; the sherbet dip of the vegetable world. And if that weren't fun enough, when you get to the prize wrapped within all those escalloped leaves my little taste buds exploded in approval. There is something to the taste of an artichoke heart that is unlike anything else on the table. If my love affair started with passion it has proceeded with even more. I grow lots of artichokes now. I still eat their leaves in just the way I used to but now I use the hearts to make a pasta sauce that has become one of our favourites.

I love their glaucous blue, extravagant, exploding foliage, so they are in the rose garden, naturally they are in the vege-table garden, but to be honest there are stands growing beside the pond in the wildlife garden and I even have clutches of them growing alongside grass paths in the meadow! A stand of artichokes in the middle of a lawn might sound odd, but why?

We remove their flower heads to eat but it would be a terrible error to grow artichokes and never allow one to flower. It would be like living next to the Uffizi and never visiting. For sheer drama and hutzpah there is nothing like an artichoke in full flower. But there is something transcendent about the iridescent blue of the beard, almost spookily so, and it sends a clarion call to the garden's bees who won't, perhaps can't, leave the flowers alone. I really don't know why more people don't grow artichokes and I don't know why they aren't more commonly grown not just for their foliage but for their flowers.

There are two ways to start artichokes; either from rooted cuttings that you buy in pots from the nursery and can treat like any container grown plant or from seed. If you don't have any growing already (throwing up material from which you can grab a rooted cutting in the autumn or spring) and you just want a couple of plants for the vegetable garden it is probably best to buy a few plants from a plant nursery rather than bring a few on from seed. This is because when you grow them from seed you can get variety in the quality of the plants that ensue.

Artichokes want a fertile well-drained spot with good amounts of sun. As such it is best to plant them into soil that has been enriched with compost and leavened with horticultural grit. They will want some protection in the winter from frost and a covering of compost applied in the autumn will do the trick. Sometimes their foliage can be punished by a frost which can cause panic but mine always push up again shortly thereafter. They start into growth nice and early in the spring which further builds the case for using them for their foliage.

151

Rhubarb

Like asparagus and purple sprouting broccoli, rhubarb marks the arrival of spring. Whilst my wife and I love the mix of astringent and sweet that it provides our children don't so they get theirs mixed into sweet and indulgent fools (perhaps a more accurate description of their parents). Many people force rhubarb which involves putting a pot (or a dustbin, frankly), weighted with a stone, over the plants in early spring to provoke an early harvest. I like rhubarb, but I am content to eat it when it is ready, so I don't bother with that.

Rhubarb is another one of these plants whose visual impact is often neglected by gardeners. Actually, a healthy fulsome stand of rhubarb is as handsome as a healthy fulsome stand of any other plant and the varieties with dramatic red streaks make it more attractive than most; it just carries with it the dual benefit of good eating. Also, if you have never seen a rhubarb plant in flower you really must; it feels like witnessing a moment frozen in prehistory. As we exchange bunches of daffodils so the dinosaurs must surely have exchanged bunches of Jurassic rhubarb flowers. I don't say that you should grow this plant for its flowers – but you should certainly see them. Once you have seen a rhubarb plant in flower, you will know exactly what I mean.

The easiest way to start rhubarb is to buy a crown that is a few years old in a pot and plop it in the ground during the winter or in early spring. Otherwise you can buy a rhizome from a supermarket packet and plant it out directly. For some reason, and not that there is anything wrong with it, Holsteiner is the variety most often on offer on supermarket stands around here so one reason to visit a plant nursery for your rhubarb might be to widen the selection of varieties you can grow. You can start rhubarb from seed but I don't have the patience.

As with asparagus don't pick in the first season, and possibly even in the second, and thereafter leave off picking from June so the plant can recharge the goodness in its structures below soil. Clumps can become congested after five or so years and if this happens lift them in November and split off sections before replanting.

– Soft fruit –

It is worth noting that an awful lot of eating can be derived from the hedgerows and forest edges that are to be found throughout our countryside and that these (providing you have the landowner's permission) offer a dividend whose only effort is the harvest itself. Like thousands of other families up and down the country we go 'blackberrying' in the autumn. Any blackberries that remain in the basket on our return find their way into pies, jams and fruit salads.

Sloes are harvested a little later. Sloes are our native plum and they are more than a little bitter, though less so after a really hot summer. For sloe gin pierce the skin of each sloe several times with a needle and then drop them into the gin before mixing in sugar and leaving to stand in a dark place, such as the back of a kitchen cupboard. Give the mixture a shake every now and then. After three months strain off the liquid and rebottle. Stand for as long as possible before drinking. How much sugar you add is clearly a matter of preference but to my mind sloe gin wants to be sweet. I prefer sloe brandy. We still have a few bottles from batches made at the farm where I grew up some twenty years ago, not to be opened on a whim. Sweet sloe brandy is a fine thing on a winter's eve.

Fruiting trees, currants and berries all offer you the same easy harvest that you would get from a country hedge but in your own garden. What is more, the variety of soft fruit now available is truly staggering. White, red or black currants; raspberries, honeyberries or loganberries; peaches, plums or apricots: take your pick. The other exciting development is that most fruit trees are now offered on dwarfing root stock so can be grown even in relatively small gardens and relied upon not to exceed a metre or two.

The thing that tends to confuse people with soft fruit is how to prune it. In all cases pruning turns on whether the fruit in question will form on old wood (that which grew in a previous season) or only on new wood (that which grows in the current one). Most fruit forms on old wood and therefore plants should be goblet pruned. Goblet pruning means encouraging a goblet shape to increase airflow and sunlight to all parts of the plant. Aim to take out dead, diseased or crossing wood but also spurs that are growing inwards towards the centre of the imaginary goblet. On the other hand, if fruit will only form on new wood you need to prune to encourage a ready supply of new wood.

There are a few apples that will fruit only at their tips but they are unusual. The majority of apples fruit on old wood. Accordingly, the majority of apples and pears will respond well to the goblet method and pruning should happen in the winter when the trees are dormant. Plums, peaches, apricots and cherries however want only very light pruning (really just to remove dead, diseased or crossing wood) and it should be done in the early summer to avoid diseases like silver leaf. Peaches and apricots particularly want the warm-est and most sheltered spot in your garden. They blossom early, often before the insects have got going, so use a cotton bud to imitate a bee, dabbing the pollen between blossoms, to increase your yield.

Red currants and white currants should be goblet pruned but black currants will only fruit on new wood so each season you want to cut a few older stems right to the ground to encourage new growth.

Gooseberries want goblet pruning and whilst raspberries are different, they are governed by the same principle. Summer fruiting raspberries bear fruit on wood that was produced the previous year. So after they have finished fruiting find the best of the new sappy growth and tie it in to the support for the following year's crop. Autumn fruiting raspberries on the other hand produce fruit on wood that has grown in the same season, so by February you want to have cut all the previous year's stems back to the ground, to encourage new stems to grow. All raspberries will thank you for a little wood ash mixed into whatever you mulch them with. Remember blue-berries want an acidic soil though apparently honeyberries are more tolerant of an alkali soil. I haven't tried them myself yet.

The disease all gardeners dread is silver leaf because it is broadly speaking a death sentence. However, the good news is that quite often suspected silver leaf turns out to be false silver leaf. In both cases the leaves take on a silvery appearance but in the case of real silver leaf this is accompanied by a black streak running through the inside of the wood which is clearly visible at pruning time.

One common problem encountered in home orchards is biannual cropping. Apple trees that are stressed or left to get out of shape can fall into the habit of producing a very light harvest in one year followed by a very heavy one the year after. The best solution is to put the trees back on a proper regime of winter pruning and spring feeding with mulch, though an orchard that is too far gone may not come readily to heel.

– Essential herbs –

Ilove herbs as much as anything else in my garden. If it is true that it makes sense to site a vegetable garden as close to the external door that is closest to the kitchen as possible, how much truer for a herb garden. The joy of popping out on a summer's morning for a handful of coriander, or chive, or parsley (or all three) to shove into a cheesy omelette makes growing herbs a must for me.

The Mediterranean herbs (like rosemary, sage, thyme and oregano) coming as they do from cracks and crevices in a rocky arid landscape, do not require the meaty nutrient rich soil of most vegetables so if you have allocated a plot close to the back door you can generally site the herb garden on the part with the poorest, sharpest draining soil. Some herbs, notably parsley and for that matter basil, do like a nutrient rich soil, so these areas can be enriched accordingly.

You will be surprised, if you are not familiar with such things already, how wide and varied are the varieties of herb on offer. From lemon basil to chocolate mint, the UK's plant nurseries can cater to your needs.

Every year, sometime in April, I go out into the garden and come back with a huge bag that is half parsley and half French tarragon, chive, mint and coriander. I then use a large sharp pair of scissors to chop the whole lot up and we eat it as a sort of English garden tabbouleh for lunch with a simple lemon juice based dressing. There is something about that first lunch that seems to change everything. Fresh new season growth, unsullied by wind, rain or sun has a sort of essential cleanness. A minerality and depth of flavour that I can't find the words to express other than to say it is the eating equivalent of a clear running highland stream.

Even if they weren't useful in the kitchen I would grow herbs for their aesthetic appeal and scent, but when it comes to eating them one of the great drivers for me is that it is so hard to buy a large enough quantity of any given herb fresh from a supermarket. The pots strike me as somewhat anaemic, but in any case there isn't enough of the herb in a single pot to furnish even one lunch in this house.

There is fun to be had too. Why not dedicate a corner of the herb garden to tisanes? Lemon verbena, camomile, and certain scented geraniums are all quite possible and, in fact, quite easy. To have a bed made over to the drinking of tisane is a rather indulgent but wonderful idea and is something I am working up in my own garden at the moment.

However, parsley is the herb that gets the most use in our household, not least because it stands and is therefore available to pick all winter. It is worth noting that herbs can be frozen for winter use if you wish. One method is to whizz them first, then push them into the pockets of an ice cube tray and cover with a little boiling water. Once frozen the cubes can be popped out into individual bags. After parsley coriander, chives, mint and rosemary find their way into the kitchen most often. I am always on the lookout for a new and useful way to employ herbs. A friend recently taught me that there is no way to improve the taste of water more than by adding rosemary! After breakfast put a few slices of lemon and a big sprig of rosemary into a large jug of water. By lunchtime it will be ready. He was right. Though simple, once tried there is no going back.

Parsley

Parsley is the most consistently useful herb in our arsenal. It can be used as tradition dictates in a white sauce to put with ham but almost all meat and fish dishes will benefit from a sprig of parsley. Moreover, it has a cleansing taste such that as you eat it you can almost feel it doing you good. One of the reasons parsley is so useful is because it remains standing through the winter and often on a frosty morning I will wrap myself in my dressing gown and steal outside to grab a sprig or two for my eggs at breakfast.

There are two types of parsley: flat leaved and curly. Everyone says the flat leaved stuff has a better flavour, and on the whole they are right, but no one points out that curly parsley has a better texture and I absolutely love it.

I have started parsley in trays before to steal a march on the season ahead and this is quite a good system. Let them grow on in their trays in the cold frame before planting them directly out, as you would with lettuce. But the easiest method is to sow direct into some freshly raked soil sometime in April or May and then thin out as you go. You can scatter the seed or sow into shallow drills made with your thumbnail. It is also worth sowing directly in August for a fresh winter crop. Parsley is a slow starter but quite hardy so any seedlings won't be troubled by a late frost. The traditional advice is to water the seed immediately with near boiling water.

Parsley is quite a hungry plant and like basil best grown in a shrubby sort of way so I always try to give each plant more space to itself than even I am comfortable with (even a couple of hands). However, if used as an edging for a vegetable bed (a use I am extremely keen on) I grow them in quite cramped conditions so they stay lower and more compact (several plants per hand).

Mint

After parsley mint is the second most used herb in our household though unlike parsley, mint doesn't stand through winter. Many things, from a bowl of vanilla ice cream to a plate of new potatoes, benefit from a pinch of mint and mint is, of course, very easy to grow. In fact unless carefully handled it can quite easily and quickly become a weed. Sadly sections long ago escaped into the rose garden and whilst its essential oils are good at warding off insect pests, every year I have to dig clumps out or it would completely take over and there would be nothing other than the roses growing through it.

The easiest way to control mint is to plant it into the ground buried in a large pot to discourage the creep of its roots sideways under the soil. Another solution, which is what we do here, is to give it a bed of its own. It will tolerate some shade and seems to like a long cool root run and water. To achieve this I have mine growing in a double raised bed (two scaffolding boards high). That said, mint requires next to no care. Cut its spent stems back to near soil level and watch the lush new growth appear in the spring. It is basically bulletproof. Over time, if patches in the middle of the clump seem to die, lift and divide to refresh it.

There are a huge number of varieties of mint, with some suggesting lemon, others chocolate and one even pineapple, but having played around with various ones I now just grow ordinary garden mint from a strain I know to smell strong and good. You have to simplify certain areas of your life and mint is one area where I have done just that.

Coriander

Coriander is easy to start from seed though does benefit from a properly warmed soil. Despite its association with dishes like Thai Green Curry it is hardier than you think once grown and will stand all through the winter; at least mine up here on a hill in Essex does. Rocket stands well through winter too. It isn't at its best from the point of view of human consumption but I start a patch of both coriander and rocket at the end of the summer in order to supplement my chicken feed. I am still lobbing them plants in February and one little red hen I have, one of the original chicks that we hatched from an egg, loves salad more than anything else.

Through a dark irony, coriander is of course best known for its association with chicken dishes but I find handfuls of the citrusy fresh herb useful for omelettes, salads and mayonnaise. The key as with so many herbs is that they have to be used very liberally.

Coriander is as easy as can be. Just walk to a bare patch of recently raked earth and gently press the relatively large seeds into the soil in a line. Push them in so they are just covered. Sow seeds every few inches, water and wait. When they start to grow, thin them out so you are left with a strong plant a minimum of a fully extended hand apart from the next strong plant. Harvest at will. Boom. So easy.

Chives

Like mint, and unlike the Mediterranean or Asian herbs, chives are native to the UK. They like a rich soil and a ready supply of water and, unsurprisingly, in our hallowed isles, can withstand a little shade. I have escapees growing strongly under a sixty-foot stretch of mature guelder rose hedge.

In addition to the standard garden form, which is well worth growing and easy to start from seed, you can grow garlic chives, which I have found to be quite rust resistant and which also genuinely taste garlicky, and also other oddities like welsh onions; which are not quite chives at all but can be treated as if they were.

Chives will be quite happy in a pot or window box but equally, you could dedicate four or five feet to them like I do. Their flowers are attractive and can be used to garnish a salad. Every part of the chive, including the bulb, is edible. Chives are more prone to rust if they are in an overcrowded spot. I have remedied rust, at least temporarily, by simply cutting the lot to the ground in order to benefit from a rush of rust free regrowth.

The easiest way to start chives is to sow them direct in the spring; alternatively start them in a seed tray inside in March. Prick them out into their own pots or, as I do, leave them in the seed tray and then attempt to plant the contents of the tray together, as if the tray were a large single pot.

Basil

Basil is unquestionably the herb over which I get most excited. Every year I grow a big block of it next to the tomatoes and I simply love the freedom of having masses of it to cut into salads, pastas and over pizzas – without feeling you are on a tight rein. It also makes a very good base flavour for a paste that I make to insert into larger vegetables (squashes or courgettes) that I am baking. Finally it is an excellent herb to cook simply with fish. Just cut long stems and fry them with the fish in olive oil. Fresh, pungent, outdoor grown basil tastes different even to the living stuff you buy in supermarkets. It tastes completely different to the dried stuff you get in jars. It has the signature basil taste but with a sort of not quite aniseed ringing clarity over the top.

The only limiting factor is our climate. As a result you can sow the seeds direct after the last frost but because I am so keen on basil I start it earlier inside in trays. I have found that if I prick the seedlings out and pot them on I often lose them to damping off (when a seedling fails due to too much moisture) so now I just leave them in their trays until things warm up at the end of April or start of May. Then I prick them directly out from the tray into the soil and put a bell cloche over them to protect them whilst they get going and the risk of frost recedes. If you can remember to, it is best to place these cloches out a week or so before planting to warm up the soil you will plant into.

I grow the plants on with plenty of room, a good hand or two between individuals, and keep them well watered. They grow in a shrubby manner and get quite large. As with all herbs, keeping them picked and watered helps to ward off bolting. It is possible to buy Italian seeds and these varieties are touted as having the best flavour but you can find very good varieties that have been bred for growing in Britain. I find both do the job perfectly well. I am not yet convinced that an Italian strain grown in Britain tastes quite the same as an Italian strain grown in Italy! When harvesting, snip stems just above a pair of leaves and the plant will break new growth. The flowers are attractive and edible too.

French tarragon

When I started out I knew I wanted tarragon and brought some on from a packet of seeds hastily grabbed at the nursery. At the appropriate moment I snipped off a few leaves to add to my cooking only to be most disappointed with the flavour. I had, of course, grabbed a packet of the almost taste-less though hardy Russian tarragon, when what I was after was the splendidly tasty but somewhat tender French tarragon.

As it happens (though I didn't know it at the time) the clue was in the packet of seeds because French tarragon cannot be brought on from seed (its flowers are sterile) so it must be propagated by cuttings. So if you want French tarragon the easiest method is to pick up a pot of it from the local plant nursery.

Because it is somewhat tender, I grow it in a raised bed and in the autumn I cut it back and put plastic bonnets over its various clumps in a haphazard fashion. So far it has survived my winters and come back strongly each spring. You can simply pull a couple of leaves but if you want more cut a stem above a pair of leaves and it will make new growth like basil.

French tarragon is one of the very best herbs to have in the garden and can be paired with much beyond chicken. Like basil it is one of my favourite herbs to cook with fish and also like basil I just cut long wands of it and fry it and the fish together in olive oil. Both herbs provide the fish with a pungent and delectable flavour. There is no need for anything else, except a little pepper and salt.

Rosemary

Rosemary is a Mediterranean herb and as such likes sharp drainage and good sun. Because it is evergreen it is a useful herb in the winter, best known for its pairing with lamb though we use it in the autumn just as frequently in trays of roasted vegetables. As with lavender, cuttings are easy to take in the summer so if you have one shrub it is no trouble to make more.

Rosemary makes a fine hedge and can stand on its own two feet in a shrubbery also. I have one plant that has grown taller than me. One of the reasons I would consider rosemary for a hedge is because its flowers are surprisingly beautiful and can come early in fine weather, as early as March. Also, it seems to be a whisper more assured in our climate than lavender. It is equally useful for overwintering ladybirds too.

Prostrate (or creeping) rosemary is very like its cousin but it has a distinct growth pattern, sending branches out and down in a line as straight as a die. This makes it an interesting choice to grow in a row atop a wall or in a pot as it has a beguiling and slightly startling form.

Sage

Frying a few leaves in oil as a very basic pasta sauce is one way forward but in truth sage falls into the category of herbs that I should probably use an awful lot more of than I do. Traditionally paired with pork, it has a powerful flavour that can really ground a dish. Like its cousins it enjoys sharp drainage and good sun and in fact during the winter can look very unhappy, to the point of eliciting concern, but don't fear, it can be relied upon to bounce back strongly in the spring. Sage grows slowly and patience will be required (or a large number of specimens planted) if you want to use it in any great volume.

Thyme

My favourite use for thyme is not culinary at all and I have to mention it here. *Thymus serpyllum* (snakelike, creeping thyme) is a very useful plant, a talking point and easy to bring on from seed (use the same method as for wild strawberries

165

recounted in Part I). Beyond this, growing it in a mat over ugly crazy paving, or through gravel, or in the cracks on a path or terrace can immeasurably improve an otherwise slightly dodgy part of the garden or lift an already nice part to new heights. Walking across a thick carpet of creeping thyme does absolutely no damage to the plants and releases a heady and delicious scent. If our dogs have rolled in something and I haven't time to wash them my wife makes them lie in creeping thyme. All types of thyme send up beautiful spikes of flower in the summer too.

For all these reasons *Thymus serpyllum* is a herb that you should have in your herb garden, running along or growing through its highways and byways. If you want enough plants to pepper a path the most cost-effective option is to start them from seed but it should be noted a wide range of varieties are available as pot grown specimens from most plant nurseries.

There are literally hundreds of varieties of thyme and whilst I don't believe eating any of them would do you any harm, some have been noted for their culinary use. The most popular variety is variously known as French, English or Common Thyme and because it is evergreen I have used it towards the front of my flowerbeds as an alternative to box, though it only grows to about twelve inches tall. Lemon Thyme is popular and a worthy addition to any herb garden. I have found that thyme has an authority that supersedes all other herbs; for example if you add it to a mix of herbs in a dish it is the flavour of the thyme that hits the top note. Of all the Mediterranean herbs I have found thyme especially loves sharp drainage and full sun.

Oregano

The last of our Mediterranean herbs. Like the others it wants sharp drainage and full sun. It is easy to bring on from seed in the spring and is perennial, so if you start a decently sized pot it will hang around happily for several years. As with sage I don't use oregano nearly enough, but it is a killer addition to pizza and a very sound addition to fried eggs.

In Britain, oregano is often called marjoram which can cause more than a little confusion – so I will clear the matter up for you. Whilst oregano is commonly thought of as a Mediterranean herb it is in fact native to Britain too where it grows on verges and in grass. If you walk past a clump in the summer it smells lovely. Wild marjoram is a perfectly useable herb (it is the same herb, *Origanum vulgare*) though it is reckoned the Mediterranean strains taste better!

– Companion planting and edible flowers –

Companion planting is the basic idea that growing certain crops close to each other holds benefits that exceed the sum of their parts. This might be because one crop 'protects' the other from pests and disease (through, for example, acting as sacrificial decoy or as a repellent) or because the two crops benefit from each other symbiotically in some other dimly understood way. Companion planting doesn't have to be strictly species specific either; for example, merely having flowers in the vegetable patch is a good idea because it will attract pollinators, but when such flowers can deter pests and sometimes even have a legitimate role in the kitchen themselves the pairing becomes almost irresistible.

I have a friend who is a keen gardener and the thing that struck me most after my first visit to her utterly lovely garden was the sheer volume of flowers she uses in her food. Perhaps in a typical masculine way (and after my own not entirely successful attempt at lavender bread twenty years previously) I had discounted the value of flowers in the kitchen, thinking them possibly rather silly or some sort of afterthought. But my friend seemed to use them in a way that was integral; from the tart floral salad, to the loaf of bread to the lavendered butter. Everything somehow had the influence of flowers or herbs not upon it so much as within it, and it gradually dawned on me how much flowers and herbs can add to a vegetable patch.

For example nasturtiums are a good sacrificial crop for slug prone vegetables, but they will also lend salad a good peppery kick or garnish a cake with aplomb. The flowers of violets and forget-me-nots will attract pollinators but also perfect a salad. And who would think of adding sunflower petals to fried fish for a nice nutty flavour? However, of all flowers marigolds are the ones that perhaps most belong in a vegetable garden.

Marigolds can confuse the uninitiated. There are in fact two families of plants commonly used in English gardens called 'marigolds'. *Calendula officinalis*, the old world marigold from somewhere in the Mediterranean basin, is the herb that is said, when in a cream, to be good for nappy rash. It can also be used as a saffron substitute, for example to colour rice. Tagetes, the showier new world marigold from Mexico is said to be a natural insect repellent and is therefore well worth planting near tomatoes. Despite coming from Mexico, tagetes is usually called a 'French' marigold. The 'African' marigold, also sometimes seen, is its cousin.

The name marigold is of course derived from Mary's Gold, and whatever one you grow it is easy to see why. I consider the French marigolds, the ones with deep crimson petals and gold lacing, to be things of extreme beauty, but all are worth growing.

Chives are good at deterring pests from roses and they flower nicely anyway and so look perfectly appropriate in a rose garden. As mentioned, I often try to grow tomatoes in a patch where garlic grew recently. You also already know I grow basil in close proximity to tomatoes not just because it is said to improve their flavour, but because it is a convenient pairing when it comes to lunch. And you also already know that I am keen on using parsley to edge vegetable beds, and one reason for this is because I suspect its strong scent might keep pests away. I can't prove it, but it is my view.

Anyway, the idea of a vegetable garden being no more than boring rows of vegetables has, I think, finally been rejected. Flowers and herbs should wind their merry way through any vegetable patch, not just in order to support the vegetables, not just to attract pollinators or repel pests, but very often because they have their own distinct contribution to make to the kitchen table too.

– Concluding Part IV –

Having read this chapter I hope you are fizzing with plans for your own patch and inspired to furnish many meals to come. There is no pleasure quite like growing your own food and no delight quite like sharing it with your family or friends. I hope you are excited about thinking, in this area of your garden at least, a little bit more like a chef and a little bit less like a gardener.

My advice, already forcefully delivered, is that the place to grow things that are destined for the kitchen is as near as possible to the external door closest to the kitchen itself. But if your vegetable patch is a window box, choose the sunniest sill closest to the kitchen sink and if you do nothing else, grow some indoor windowsill basil – and I bet once you've started it will become a habit for life.

In addition to growing out, think hard about what could be persuaded to grow up. A kiwi scrambling up a drain pipe? A vine straddling a shed? If you need a hedge anyway why not make it an edible one (chock-full of crab apples, plums, nuts and black currants that will produce a harvest that can either be eaten fresh or made into delicious jams) and if you fancy a flowering tree why not make sure it is one that will bear a fruit you like to eat in the autumn. Even a length of guttering attached to a wall is a useful place to sow the odd salad leaf or herb.

If I can leave you with one parting shot it would be this: vegetable growing should, in my opinion, be undertaken without too much agitation about the rules and with a certain level of Heath Robinsonesque abandon. Give yourself permission to try something just because it feels like a good idea, and be prepared to sacrifice a certain amount of tidiness for what must always remain the overall objective: a delicious meal.

Part V

Trees & hedges

– Trees and all that crawl within them –

Being civilised is planting trees even if you won't be around to enjoy them. To lose hold of this is surely to disappear into a black hole of self from which it is hard to emerge. And yet, as a species, we seem to be leaving our environment in a far more shabby state than we found it. I worry about climate change (manmade or otherwise) though plastic in the ocean makes me sadder because it is just such a hideous and visible manifestation of what cretins we can be. Seeing all those plastic toothbrushes and crisp packets swirling round is like coming face to face with our own mindlessness. It is to have our collective stupidity paraded in front of us. It is embarrassing. It makes me feel queasy. As a species we have been busted by our headmaster and he is tut tutting as he pulls back the cover to find our stash of illicit sweets.

And what about the gulls and fish with twenty different ghastly pieces of plastic in their stomachs? And what of the micro plastics that we can't even see from children's games and dreadful shower gel (I never really understood what was wrong with a bar of soap, preferably one that smells of tar). However, the thing that I consider to be the most worrying is the wholesale disappearance of insects. People don't seem to understand that without insects plants can't pollinate and without pollination we can't eat. Trashing the place is one thing but if people start to get hungry it will become a whole different matter.

Einstein reputedly said that if bees ever disappeared he would give the human race four years. Any gardener who grows a peach tree knows that without insects you don't get pollination and therefore you don't get peaches. This is because in Britain, peach trees blossom early, before the bulk of our insects have massed from under their winter blanket, so if you don't move from blossom to blossom with a cotton bud imitating the action of a bee, you get no crop. If you forget and you get a couple of peaches it is because the period of blossoming just about coincided with a few early insects, if you get none it didn't. Now apply that to maincrops of apples, pears and plums and imagine those 'grown in Britain' bags at the supermarket empty. Then think of the fields of peas and beans. Without insects not only could we not feed ourselves, we couldn't grow the crops we need to feed our animals either. Hunger sits on the other side of a world without insects.

Am I making a fuss about nothing? You judge. The latest study from Germany shows that Europe may have lost two thirds of its flying insects in the last thirty years. Insect population spread is rarely even. Rather, they mass in certain areas. If one area fails due to human encroachment, pesticide use or simply a bad winter, nature has provided resilience and the opportunity to mass back up from elsewhere. But as these insect groups get further and further apart, and the areas themselves get smaller and smaller, the ability to mass back up reduces. What is the critical point beyond which total collapse is the only outcome? What happens if next spring all the blossom comes out and there are no insects to dance across it? Your guess is as good as mine.

No one truly understands what is causing the current wholesale decline in insects though it seems to be happening all over the world. Climate change may be one part of the answer because certain insects have evolved to survive at a certain running temperature. An example is the great yellow bumblebee. This bee was once common throughout England but has been pushed further and further north to seek cooler and cooler climes. It now hangs on only in the northern tip of Scotland. As the world continues to warm there is nowhere further north for it to go because there is no further useful landmass until you get to Iceland. Climate change has pushed a number of plants and insects into making a final highland stand. God bless each and every one of them.

The blanket use of pesticides and their accrual in our hedgerows and waterways is another obstacle for insect populations. Every spring farmers cruise the fields with great sprayers and just the other day I turned the corner with the children in the car and the roof down and got a face full of the stuff. It is disgusting. I am certain enlightened descendants will look back in horror at this epoch for precisely this reason. It is not any individual farmer's fault, and sometimes we have made matters harder for them accidentally. When I was younger we used to burn stubble. Burning stubble controlled insects that would otherwise attack the next year's crop (not absolutely, but more or less). Neonicotinoid seed coverings now do the same job. What to do? None of this is easy. We must dig our way out of the hole that we are in and we must do so standing alongside farmers.

I guarantee most farmers would rather not use chemicals, but they also have their families to feed. As with defence of the realm, might this be one area where public good and government subsidy run in the same direction? Imagine if we went organic as a nation. Should we pay for this collectively? It would be a lot more useful than a great many other things we pay for collectively.

Of all nations Britain seems to be in the greatest mess, at least according to the 2016 State of Nature Report. Our islands are among the most nature depleted in the world. Is this hyperbolic? Since the war we have lost 97 per cent of our wildflower meadows. During the same period vast reams of hedgerow have been ripped out to create ever bigger fields. It is reckoned that by the mid 1990s over seventy or eighty thousand miles had been lost, enough to wrap the globe several times! From an insect's perspective its useable habitat has just melted away. Add in climate change and blanket pesticide use and is it any wonder that your car windscreen doesn't thicken with insects during the summer anymore? Come on, don't you remember the clouds of insects when we were all children? I do.

It is reckoned homeowners account for about 5 per cent of land ownership in the UK. Add to this the land that is in the ownership of the Crown, public and conservation charities and you get up to about 15 per cent. Whilst the battle could be won overnight if we helped farmers, as gardeners we can make a difference too. We can provide the little insect friendly outposts necessary so that one day insects can mass back up nationally.

I like to think of a three-point plan for insects: Water, Mess, Trees. Insects love water, insects love messy patches and above all insects love trees. It is also worth noting that our native plants will favour our native insects because they have evolved to feed off and shelter within their foliage, so native plants in your water, native mess in your garden and native trees in the ground will help insects best of all.

Of all trees, a mature oak is reckoned to be the most insect friendly. In addition to bryophytes, lichens and moss (not to mention bats, birds and mammals) a mature oak will support up to as many as 280 different types of insect. It will also sequester large quantities of carbon dioxide. Willows, birches and hawthorns are also reckoned to be particularly beneficial to insects. But only about 13 per cent of Britain is covered in forest, compared to a European average that is allegedly as high as 30 per cent. The picture here is surprisingly bleak.

On one measure all gardening comes down in the end to managing trees. In the absence of grazing animals, any garden abandoned would simply revert to some form of woodland. But of course there have always been grazing animals and so it is most likely that Britain prior to hominid incursion was a blend of woodland and pasture; a battle between tree and aurochs. Our native insects evolved over millions of years to favour this mixed habitat.

Recognising that as gardeners we are simply standing in the way of woodland can help us garden better. There is a basic end state towards which our arboreal friends will develop if they are not checked by us or by marauding herbivores. How and when we check this progress towards woodland is how we shield and subdivide our garden, it is how we introduce many vertical layers and it is how we control what will grow in the clearings between.

– *How to plant a tree* –

When you choose a tree at a plant nursery it is worth taking a moment to look at its structure and shape. Don't just grab the first one in the row. The structure and shape of the tree you buy will be the foundation for the tree you end up with. You might want multiple stems and a complicated patina, or you might want a section of long clear stem (a standard); either way it is best to try to start as you mean to go on.

Once you have the tree home the whole question of planting looms. People have different approaches to planting trees and in fact methods can vary quite widely so here is what I do:

- Water the tree a good hour before planting.
- If planting into grass, remove the top soil around the tree in a circle or square roughly three feet in diameter.
- Dig a hole that is double the circumference of the pot in question. Really, the more soil you break up around where the tree is to be planted the better, but this is limited by the time available for the job. I generally dig square holes rather than round ones so that eventually the tree's roots can find a corner and break out, rather than spiralling round. This is especially worthwhile if you have heavy soil.

- I generally do not add compost or food, preferring instead that the tree quickly adapts to the soil into which it is being planted rather than living for a period off a false bounty.
- If the tree in question wants sharp drainage and you garden on heavy soil plant it on a bed of horticultural grit. I have sometimes placed a layer of larger stones below the grit where it has seemed sensible to do so.
- Once the pot is off the tree gently stroke the roots so that they are pointing out into what will be the neighbouring soil rather than along what was the side of a pot.
- Once the tree is standing in the hole, back fill with the spoil that you have dug, breaking it up further as you go.
- Firm the soil in around the newly planted tree lightly with your boot, toe pointed at the trunk so you step evenly on plant and soil. As with other plants water thoroughly.

If possible I do not stake trees because if you ever intend to take the stake off it will be like a patient with a broken leg who has her crutches kicked away from under her. That said, parts of my garden are windy and in these places I use an iron fencing pin plunged into the soil angled in the direction of the prevailing wind, so the weather blows off the trunk, rather than against it. Iron fencing pins are good because they have a level of give, meaning that whilst they support the tree they don't do all the work for it.

I tie the trunk to the iron fencing pin using garden string but knot it so that the string provides a buffer to the stake to prevent direct rubbing on the bark. These ties are replaced every year, usually in time for the autumn winds. After planting I provide a good thick mulch of compost and this mulch is replaced and the area weeded each spring until the tree is established. Remember that newly planted trees will need regular watering during the summer for their first few seasons. I think trees are best planted in the autumn so that they can make the most of the following spring the moment it arrives. Trees planted in the autumn tend to need less watering the following summer. Whips on the other hand can be planted anytime over the winter right up to March or April.

A 'whip' is merely a tree in its first few years of life. Whips are cheaper to buy than larger trees in containers because they are merely lifted from a field at the nursery and posted to your door. Many people say it is actually better to start with a whip than with a tree because it will grow away faster having been moved younger. I am not sure this is always the case, particularly if a more mature tree comes from a reputable nursery and it isn't pot bound. But it is certainly cheaper to plant whips, particularly if you intend to plant in large numbers. The method for a hedge is to remove the turf in the line of a trench at least three feet across and then break up the soil. Some people just make a slit with a spade and slide the whip's roots into it before firming with their boot. If I have the time I tend to take the trouble to dig a little hole and spread its roots out.

People don't often think of planting whips if they are planting a single tree but there is no reason (other than having to wait longer for it to reach maturity) why you shouldn't use a whip. I have. When you think the average whip might cost forty pence it's a super cheap way of starting a tree. I planted a single hornbeam that way four years ago and it's now considerably taller than me.

– Trees of the British countryside –

In some way all trees make a visual rhyme; they fall on a scale somewhere between order and chaos. There is a sort of play off in life between regularity and irregularity. If everything is too far in either direction there is a sense of strain, while the place in the middle of the two seems to be where real beauty lies. Mess brings haunting romance, order reminds us the ground under our feet is solid; between the two is the real, immediate captivating business of life.

And this is a song that the trees sing too. The rigour and symmetry of a Christmas tree versus the collapsed mess of a weeping ash. The common ash, for example, sits somewhere in the middle, as did the mature elms of old. An oak perhaps has an ounce more rigour than an ash, and a mature elm an ounce less, but anyone who looks at trees regularly will know what I am trying to get at.

The Ash family – Fraxinus

The ash is one of the greatest English trees, if not the greatest English tree. I think of ashes towering above hedgerows or peppering the side of a wood with their knowing canopy, as beautiful in winter as in summer. Their leaves don't amount to much taken individually but taken together they paint a million little brush strokes in the sky. Trying to identify trees from their twigs in winter is a fun game to play (if you like such things) but the ash with its strong coal black eyes is the easiest of them all. Once you have identified an ash twig you will never fail to notice one again. Ash is a very fine wood. The best for burning as it fills the room with a sweet unmistakable fragrance.

The Beech family – Fagus

Beech trees are, for a reason that is not immediately obvious, stately. They have, to my mind, more symmetry and rigour than either ash or oak, but they also seem to hold themselves in a way that is impervious to you as the observer. They don't quite invite you in as an oak tree does, but neither do they turn you out; they stand defiant. The unique selling point of a beech tree is that whilst it is deciduous, it holds its leaves through the winter. Before winter sets in the leaves scorch a bright golden orange. For a moment in the autumn beeches sing a fiery song that has no parallel. Beech sometimes isn't keen on a heavy soil so if you garden on clay consider hornbeam.

The Chestnuts – Castanea sativa and Aesculus hippocastanum

Chestnuts come in two varieties, sweet (*Castanea sativa*) and horse (*Aesculus hippocastanum*). Both sit within the wider fagus family of the beeches but for practical purposes they are stand-alone trees in the English landscape. Both trees are French imports from the seventeenth century and not English, in the native sense, at all. The horse chestnut is of course the giver of conkers whilst the sweet chestnut is responsible for those stalls that sell us bags of warm nuts at Christmas on Oxford Street.

The sweet chestnuts around here seem to keep their leaves longer than other trees and this makes a mature specimen really stand out on a woodland edge at the change of the seasons. The horse chestnut on the other hand is one of the world's great flowering trees. Whilst in full flow in May its exotic fecundity is hard to match and it carries all the promise of an evening spent in Paris during a misspent and foolish youth.

Horse chestnuts will flower in either white or a sort of high pink to crimson. The white flowers have within them dashes of pink and they are preferable to my eye. If they aren't fiddled around with they will make very dense and interesting crowns in old age. They also make lots of mess. Their leaves are slow to compost and their conkers a bore to pick up. Plant one for the sheer love of the flowering, which is unbeatable, or not at all.

The Holly family – Ilex

Some trees that are commonly thought of as best for hedges actually make very appealing specimens if given enough space. Holly will fulfil the role of a hedge quite happily in a small garden, but given their head they will make ravishing specimen trees. A mature holly won't make a great height and you don't need a garden measured in acres to grow one.

In my experience hollies don't like being moved (I have moved one successfully but it complained terribly and almost died) so try to choose the right spot first time round. With a good clean stem to about six feet, and then a dense canopy, the holly tree is possibly my favourite of all.

Hollies bear male and female flowers on separate trees and so if you plant a single holly (say a female) and have no male nearby you might be disappointed when you get no berries. For lots of berries it is necessary to plant lots of trees (or as a minimum, one male and one female) but a holly hedge near to a holly tree should do the trick.

The Oak family – Quercus

There are in fact several different types of oak. The common oak is the one most visible in my part of the country but in the north west the sessile oak is more common. Both types perform the same highly beneficial role for wildlife. In addition to the common and sessile oak there are Turkey oaks (whose branches tend to point up towards the sky) and evergreen Holm oaks. Last summer a friend of mine poured me a glass of acorn wine. I accepted it politely but expected it to be disgusting. It sat pale and waxy and chilled in the glass. It was exquisite.

The Lime family – Tilia

Lime trees are famous for providing giant sweeping avenues that approach stately homes and in this role they perform well. Their sweet-scented sticky flowers attract droves of bees in spring. There are large-leaved limes and small-leaved limes which have distinct territories within the British Isles and the common lime which is a hybrid of the two. Lime trees famously sucker like mad around the base of their trunks, no doubt to the chagrin of many aristocrats' gardeners.

Maple – Acer

The common field maple is our native member of the acer family. Unsurprisingly therefore its principal aesthetic contribution is via the colour of its leaves which go a bright canary yellow in the autumn, particularly after a hot summer. With its distinctive five lobed leaf and helicopter seed pods it is unmistakable, and in the part of the country in which I live is the commonest hedge along with elm, which also goes canary yellow in the autumn, meaning the countryside lights up each year in October.

There are other maples in the English countryside, including the Norway maple with its distinct red leaves. Field maples are occasionally allowed by farmers to break the line of a hedge and make for a fine if somehow slightly squat crown. The trees generally carry with them a sort of pleasing agricultural stolidness.

Birch – Betula

The Jacquemontii birch has a very appealing white papery bark that peels off as the tree grows larger. It is certainly an arresting specimen tree for a garden and provides a dose of visual interest during the otherwise drab winter months. There are garden varieties of birch that will weep too. Despite their association with gardens, birch has a valuable role to play in natural woodland. They provide an important home for fungi and also food for many moths, whilst their seeds are a staple for many birds.

Alder – Alnus

Alders set up residence close to water and sure enough, the seventy-foot alders in my garden are at the very bottom of the meadow by the brook. The trees themselves seem to grow strongly towards the sky with several trunks, perhaps because they were coppiced as much as a century ago.

However, it is the swirling catkins followed by chocolate fruit that to me are its particular crowning glory. Incidentally, don't confuse alder with the plant of the similar sounding name elder, the latter being a smaller native tree and sometime shrub which gifts us the flowers for cordial!

Willow – Salix

The willow has an unshakeable attraction to life and this is one of its defining features. If you do no more than cut a stem and plunge it into the ground the right way up nine times out of ten it will root and you will get a tree, because willows have an abundance of natural rooting hormones.

If planted by water the rate of growth can be staggering, something that has long been understood and in fact is noted in the book of Isaiah. This unstoppable capacity for growth makes it a good tree for coppicing. One word of caution: willow's almost unstoppable rate of growth both above and below ground makes them an enemy to both drains and soakaways.

My part of North Essex is associated with the cricket bat willow, and the larger share of the damp fertile meadows that adjoin the Colne and Stour rivers are given over to their production. Willows, and of all willows particularly the weeping willow, are associated with the water's edge and no tree reflects more gracefully in the water's surface under the influence of a gentle summer's breeze.

The Poplar family – Populus

My father was sniffy about the Lombardy poplar, which is the tall fastigiate version of the tree (meaning it grows straight up like a pencil) and is very typical of North Essex. They give the longer views from this garden a Tuscan feel on a baking hot summer's day.

The genetic story behind the poplars is somewhat confusing. Our native poplar is the black poplar. The Lombardy poplar is its cousin. However, various introductions and hybrids have arrived or been cultivated and now the field of poplars is quite broad and even complex. Simplest to think of them as follows: the native black poplar, the Lombardy, the white poplars, the grey poplars, aspens and the balsam poplar which unsurprisingly smells pleasant.

The white poplar is a remarkably beautiful tree that bares, if the wind blows, the silver undersides of its leaves, which from a distance look like a thousand little polished buttons dancing in the air. Once seen never forgotten – and I couldn't recommend this tree more highly on this basis. It suckers very readily and I am using this to my advantage as I allow a hedge of it to spring up a stone's throw from the mother tree.

The Walnut – Juglans

People are surprised to learn that it is perfectly possible to harvest a crop of walnuts in the UK. However, if you want a crop you will have to have more than one walnut tree growing in your garden. I have three, each about thirty yards from the next, and they all crop perfectly well. Walnuts seem to like our climate with its relatively large number of sunshine hours and relatively light rainfall. They are said to like a relatively alkaline soil without too much sand or clay but they thrive here.

Whilst walnuts are not typical of English forests they are dotted about the countryside. It is worth noting that all trees grown in close proximity (as is typical in a forest setting with a closed canopy) will grow taller and thinner for the light than if they can proceed in splendid isolation. Walnut is no exception. As such, to get a sense of what a walnut really has

189

to offer you need one, typically in a garden, growing on its own. In this setting the crowns grow in a particularly beautiful and pleasing way on top of attractive stout trunks. The leaves are not remarkable.

The common walnut can be mistaken for the black walnut, an American import from the seventeenth century. The black walnut has a darker bark and larger foliage. It also releases a chemical in the soil at its roots that inhibits the growth of other plants. Whilst this is a very clever strategy from the tree's perspective (self-weeding) exercise caution if you intend to plant other things close to it! Walnuts don't seem to enjoy very great longevity; sometimes they just tire and die.

Wild Cherry – Prunus

Showy garden varieties of cherry are best known for their extravagant spring blossom, but wild cherries blossom in an equally rumbustious manner. Cherries seem to like our patch of North Essex, I think because of the high level of chalk in the soil, and they pepper our hedges and woodlands. Cherry blossom is somehow both bold and delicate at the same time and the combination of characteristics startles.

But the appeal of cherry trees travels further than their spring blossom: they all have fascinating bark peppered with little eyes that continue to photosynthesise even when the tree is leafless. Whilst the leaves of most cherries are nothing to write home about, in the autumn many turn vivid scarlet and this can provide a display almost as alluring as their blossom in the spring. My wild cherries sport an abundance of self-polishing bright red fruit in the autumn.

Cherries' roots travel close to the surface so if you are planting one it is best to keep the area at its base well weeded whilst it establishes. Don't pass the opportunity to plant a wild cherry if you have the space for one. Some cherries can be a little prone to canker, which causes them to ooze, and various other fungal illnesses, and so are best pruned in the summer when there are less spores about to find their way into the pruning wounds.

The Cedar family – Cedrus

There is no native cedar tree on these isles and yet the spreading boughs of the Cedar of Lebanon has become synonymous with the English country house. All cedars smell (which is why their wood was used to make trunks for cloth that would keep clothes moths off) though not being native I am not sure they make any particularly distinct contribution to our UK wildlife.

The Blue Atlas cedar is a tree that has long captivated me because of its colour. However, it quickly grows very large indeed. Here I garden over five acres and I am not certain I have the space for one! There is a spot I have in mind but the matter is still very much under debate. When I say the tree needs space I really mean it.

– Trees for a smaller garden –

Sometimes, in a smaller garden, you just want an interesting tree for a corner or to frame a view. In our garden in London we had a weeping pear in one corner. It performed its job reasonably well. In fact there are a very large number of smaller trees that have been bred specifically for garden use.

A fruit tree

Many fruit trees are now being grafted onto dwarfing stock with the smaller garden in mind. This means their natural vigour is reduced and they can be relied upon to stick to not much more than six feet or so in height. If you want something that will flower in the spring but also feed you in the autumn check the catalogues for an apple or pear tree on dwarfing stock.

Showy cherry

There are a great number of smaller cherry trees available and really it is a question of taking your pick. I am particularly fond of *Prunus incisa* The Bride for its crystal white papery blossom with a slight scarlet eye. It is the tree I chose for the central avenue in my garden. The cherry tree

Tai-haku is another fine variety with white blossom; it may grow a little taller. Over time many cherries will achieve a comfortable spreading habit that is quite distinct and very attractive. Amanogawa is one cherry that doesn't because it naturally grows straight up like a pencil and therefore doesn't crowd out neighbours. For this reason it is very useful in a smaller garden, though completely lovely in a large garden too.

Crab apple

As with fruit trees on a dwarfing stock, and showy cherries, there seems to be a greater and greater selection of crab apples on offer. Some even have purple or reddish bark and they tend to have scarlet, pink or white blossom. Whichever type you grow, and however fine the blossom, the tree is celebrated most for the spectacle of its autumn fruit.

Rowan

A rowan (also known as a mountain ash) is one of the most beautiful native English trees. Better still it is a small-ish tree and even in the wild, living for several hundred years, it will never reach much beyond about fifty feet. It carries a particularly delicate white blossom and is then festooned with attractive red berries. The foliage is pinnate, which means it presents like a feather, and highly attractive.

Hazel

Few people think of hazel as 'showy' but I think it is, when festooned in catkins. Of course, it can also be regularly coppiced to control its size so that as a whole it becomes more like an attractive shrub. If you are a catkin lover, and you want some evergreen, you might otherwise consider a silver tassel bush.

– *Three trees for a pot* –

If you are thinking of putting an olive, fig or citrus in a pot you might be anxious as to what to do when the tree outgrows the pot it is in. The standard thing would be to pot it on into a larger pot. However, at some point, you don't want a still larger pot so what to do then? The answer is to lift the plant and trim its roots back by a third or so before replanting it in the pot from which it has come. I would conduct this operation during the winter in the case of a fig, but in early summer with a citrus or olive.

Trees grown in a pot will want an annual feed. The best method is to scratch away an inch or two of the surface soil in the spring and refresh it with compost. Afterwards I top dress the surface of all the pots here with horticultural grit, partly to keep moisture in, partly to keep weeds down but mostly because it just looks nice. Anything planted in a pot requires regular watering during the warmer half of the year.

Olive

Olives are generally far tougher than people think and can be grown as specimens or even hedges. I have planted several here in the garden. I love their dancing silver green foliage. I love the fact that they are evergreen. If you want an olive to fruit it needs some cold during the winter (but not below –10 degrees, which will damage it) and its soil shouldn't get too dry. I don't grow my olives for their fruit but for the way they create wavy blocks of off-green colour against a bright blue sky. They are very happy in a pot.

Fig

I completely love figs and now grow at least ten different varieties in this garden. I don't grow them for the fruit (though I don't turn my nose up at it either) but I grow them for their foliage. For outdoor planting it is generally held that Brown Turkey is the most reliable cropper in our climate. Figs need to have their roots restricted if you wish them to fruit heavily and of course this happens automatically in a pot.

Citrus

I was given a citrus tree by a friend and I have nurtured it faithfully over several years. It is placed out in the garden in its pot after the last frost and dutifully returned to the house before the first one. Very unusually citrus bear both fruit and flower at the same time, which is what makes Seville with its oranges such a sweet-smelling spectacle. The only trouble with my citrus (it is some sort of lemon kumquat cross) is that the fruit it produces is as bitter as a fishwife's gossip and entirely unusable.

– Evergreens for any size of garden –

Topiary (shaping the dense green foliage of evergreens) can, in the largest or smallest of gardens, add either jovial lightness (creating the visual equivalent of a good joke) or impart an air of extraordinary formality. It is an art form and is one of several things we have in common with the other great gardening nation, Japan. Though in Japan they do it slightly differently.

Where topiary stops and merely cutting the hedge starts is a fine line. For example cloud pruning a hedge, which the Japanese are masters at, is of course topiary every bit as much as growing the outline of a spaniel digging in the garden. The former practice, a sort of hazy shaping which seems to listen in some way to what the plant is doing, but just gives it cleaner lines as it does it, is more exciting to me. Box cats and chickens are fun and different geometric shapes can speak volumes in a garden, but it is when you listen to the plant itself, and some sort of partnership evolves between the snipper and the snipped, that I get most excited. At its best this is the path to creating continuing lines of green that sit in the landscape like threads of visual cashmere.

Box is the go-to plant for topiary and edges. The presence first of box blight, and more recently a nasty caterpillar that is spreading out of the south east and devours the foliage, sometimes the whole lot over the course of a single night, has made growing box a somewhat risky business. Forgetting the caterpillar issue for a moment, the flood of panic that accompanied the onset of box blight has abated somewhat in the last couple of years. Growing box in positions where it gets good ventilation together with keeping it well fed and watered seems to offer some glimmer of hope. Furthermore, the practice of simply cutting affected plants to the ground (and burning the foliage) to watch and see if they grow back without the disease offers a second glimmer of hope.

That said, I consciously made the decision not to over rely on box in this garden because the pain of watching the whole thing melt on account of some silly blight (or caterpillar) would be too great. In some cases, where I might have grown box columns I have in fact grown yew. Holly balls can substitute for box balls and whilst it is hard to find alternatives to box for edging (because box really does stay so tight and dense even at very low levels) there are non-plant alternatives. A flowerbed can be edged with corten steel very attractively if you have the funds and, I think, quite attractively with painted scaffolding boards if you don't. In the vegetable garden beds can be edged with parsley.

That said, the various nurseries do have lists of plants that can replace box for edging but despite best efforts none is quite what box was. Sometimes I use several pieces of box to suggest a line as against a dense under-ventilated hedge, which is some sort of compromise. This practice of suggesting a line also steals less light from the bed it frames, though provides less shelter too.

Ilex crenata (Japanese holly) is often touted as the best box alternative for edging and may indeed be the closest fit. Sometimes it is better not to even attempt to grow a box lookalike but grow a different plant for its own evergreen merits. I think rosemary is a good and much underutilised hedging plant that can be kept tight-ish, flowers beautifully and delivers a splendid scent. There is no doubt however that for the purposes of topiary, box, provided it doesn't die on you, will do whatever you ask of it in a way that isn't quite replicated by any other plant.

Yew is the most serious native English evergreen and not just because of its presence in English churchyards and poisonous though alluring red berries. Oaks can live for 1,000 years but the oldest tree in Britain must be one of our yews. The Ashbrittle Yew in Somerset is a contender, another possibility would be the Llangernyw Yew in Wales or the Fortingall Yew in Perthshire. One of these trees is almost certain to be more than 4,000 years old and some have suggested as much as 9,000 years. I think that something of this informs their use in a garden. There is nothing that delivers a sense of permanence, and perhaps nothing quite so horticulturally English, as a neatly clipped yew hedge. Its dark green has the ability to pull all the frippery of a tumultuous summer border down and provide it with a solid frame. Yew hedging at six feet plus is one of the indispensable, non negotiable constituents in the palette of classical English horticulture.

The tallest yew hedge in England, or even in Europe, is outside Bathurst House in Cirencester. It is easily spotted if you walk round the town and is, in effect, a giant piece of topiary that takes several gardeners days to cut even with the aid of special platforms. But this demonstrates yew's ability to keep a disciplined shape even at great heights. Yew is an excellent choice for giant cones and baubles and Irish yew, which is fastigiate, is a fine candidate for shaggy columns. In summary, if box is the classic choice for edging and smaller more jovial pieces of topiary, yew is the go-to for hedges and larger pieces of topiary.

If you garden on heavier soil be sure to plant yew on a couple of inches of horticultural grit and if you wish for it to grow fast try to make sure you plant specimens that haven't had their leader cut.

In addition to the fact that it is well suited to being cut to fill any shape you might wish to fill, holly carries with it the promise of berries (so long as there are male and female plants about, as above). There is also something about the metallic green glimmer of a holly leaf that allows long and happy contemplation if you like such things.

Of course there are a very large number of different types of holly and these include ones with variegated (two tone) foliage, so whereas box and yew will only ever conjure their own very distinct green, holly is the first in our list that would add a splash of yellow (and a dose of chicken pox) to the giant topiary Labrador you are planning for the middle of your lawn.

Holly is not the only evergreen from a slightly left-field position that can be either used for topiary or more generally 'shaped'. Bay, Portuguese laurel and privet are worthy candidates too. Holm oak will make a very comely lollipop or block and even wild honeysuckle can be coaxed into a nice wavy form when grown as a hedge.

– *Managing trees you have inherited* –

In any new garden it is worth making an audit of what is already there (even if you have to ask a knowledgeable friend over for the purpose) and my advice would be against removing anything until you at least have a name for it. There can be a temptation to cut things down simply to place your mark on a space.

Some trees and shrubs will likely have been planted by a previous gardener but some, particularly in a slightly neglected garden, may have self-seeded or suckered and will be busy etching out a living for themselves in a place that clearly suits them. These last ones are the ones to particularly listen to because they will give you a clue about what other plants are likely to thrive in your garden and where they are likely to thrive best.

Many, many plants will break from old wood and so if a plant has lost its manners and sprawled and you are in two minds as to whether to remove it completely or not you can try giving it a severe haircut as an alternative and see how you feel about it the following year. Incidentally, if you are presented with something that you're minded to keep but that clearly needs taking back, and you are unsure by how much to take it back, quite often it can be helpful to move aside some of the foliage and look for the cutting points left by the last gardener. If in doubt, cut to this point.

In terms of maintenance, any tree or shrub that has established doesn't 'need' weeding around or mulching though mature fruit trees will still benefit from it. With the exception of fruit trees, most trees don't need routine pruning. If you have very large trees it is sensible to get them checked periodically by a tree surgeon for safety reasons, to ensure there aren't boughs that could fall from them onto someone's head.

Trees don't particularly enjoy being entirely smothered with ivy, and in extreme cases it can cause them damage. This is a balancing act though because ivy, flowering as it does during a lean time in the year, is of incomparable benefit to insects and birds and just as importantly will provide an evergreen splodge in an otherwise deciduous hedge. However, if matters are getting out of control, I find it best to cut clear segments (a hand in width) out of the stems of the ivy at or near the point where they meet the tree in early spring and let the summer heat burn the segments above this point off. Don't simply pull them off because this is very likely to damage the tree.

With some trees you may wish to make aesthetic adjustments from time to time. This should be done when they are dormant in the winter and most commonly involves removing wispy (epicormic) growth from the trunk or removing any dead or damaged branches. However, sometimes it can be worth raising the crown of a tree. There is a copper beech in my garden and I have spent five years raising its crown. Originally the crown broke from the trunk at about four feet. Each winter I take a few of the lower branches off and now it breaks at about seven feet. This can be a useful enterprise and mysteriously lift a whole corner of the garden aesthetically speaking.

– Hedging for shelter –

As has already been mentioned, in Britain the prevailing weather is from the west or south west. Atlantic weather is itself driven by the progress of the jet stream across a huge ocean. The net result is warmth and moisture flowing over the British Isles making them warmer than a continental climate in the winter, and cooler in the summer. The moderating effect of the Atlantic in the west reduces as you move eastward across the UK and where I live near Colchester it is at its faintest, resulting in generally hotter summers and cooler winters than those enjoyed in Exeter.

In my garden I have Atlantic weather as a dominant theme from the west but I also have to think about the biting northerlies and easterlies that whip in off the North Sea. Of these the worst are definitely the easterlies which can cut a person (and a garden) to the quick. People used to say that there is no higher point between the spire of King's College Chapel in Cambridge and the cathedral in St Petersburg. Whether true or not when the wind blows in from the east it can bring a level of chill to this garden not often felt in a Cornish valley!

Your garden will, depending on where it is located, be subject to the same basic weather patterns described above and it is definitely worth thinking about hedges in this context. It might be tempting to think that a nice large fence with solid wooden panels will simply eradicate the problem but sadly matters are not so simple. A solid wooden fence will act as a sail and as such, in a truly windy position, will likely fail sooner or later. But solid barriers can have an odd effect on the wind anyway, creating a dead zone and then beyond it a zone of greater turbulence. Generally, it is better to have a barrier that allows the wind through but fools it as it goes and of all of these the very best is a hedge.

As a rule of thumb any barrier to the wind will usually protect a space eight times its own height horizontally, though if the land is sloping upwards this will be reduced and if the land is sloping downwards it will be increased. Without the shelter afforded by hedging, wind will run over your garden like an invading army and has the potential to undo even the most carefully laid plans. Not only will wind rock a plant, potentially to death, but it will greatly magnify the damaging effects of cold. Minus five is one thing, but minus five under the withering effect of an easterly straight from the Urals is quite another.

I have found a dense hedge of hawthorn to be the most effective fool to the wind. I suspect this is one reason why hawthorn has long been the favourite of farmers. Large dense clumps of evergreen can also provide very considerable shelter. The trouble with large dense clumps of evergreen is that they also cast lots of shade, but not, if you think about it, in the northern hemisphere along a northern boundary. As a result I have used hawthorn along our southern and western boundaries and a twenty-foot high run of cherry and Portuguese laurel to block out the northerlies and easterlies. If your garden (and neighbours) allow for it I suggest you consider some sort of similar arrangement.

– How long will my hedge take to grow? –

Once hedges have become established, they will very often throw out a relatively consistent rate of growth each season, assuming they receive a similar amount of sun and water. Often the speed to maturity is one factor when deciding what hedge to plant. Yew is often held up as an example of a slow growing plant. But, if you select plants that have not had their leader cut (the main growing stem) it might push out ten inches of growth in a single season. On the other hand, if it doesn't like the position into which it has been planted, or if you buy a plant from which the leader has been snipped, you might be lucky to get three or four inches.

At the other end of the spectrum, willow planted in nice damp soil might throw out forty inches of growth a year, or very much more once it is established. But plant it in a dry arid soil and you will get nothing like that. Leylandii is generally considered the fastest of all hedging plants and as close to inde-structible as a hedge can get. I have found this to be an accurate description, but that doesn't mean the plant doesn't have specific needs. Cutting it too much, or cutting it in the winter, or cutting it too far back can weaken the plant and leave not just brown patches but an infestation of Cypress aphid!

Finally, keeping the area around the base of a hedge well weeded will clearly increase the chances of its maturing swiftly. This can be done by planting into some landscape fabric or by mulching. The table below is a rough guide based on my experience in this particular garden. My estimates have been worked out with the help of the tape measure from my wife's sewing box, my mind's eye and occasional sallies out into the garden to measure sappy growth. Clearly the whole business is very variable, but broadly speaking I think what follows is decent for the purposes of a rough guide.

Hedging type	Notes, including approximate rate of growth
Beech	Deciduous, though retains many of its leaves through winter. Medium, about 12 inches a year. More as it establishes.
Box	Evergreen. Suitable for formal hedge. Slow growth rate, 5 inches a year, less whilst it is establishing, more after it has.
Deciduous hedging mix (elm, field maple, dog rose etc)	Deciduous. Informal hedge. Quite fast, from 12 to 20 inches a year, more when it gets going.
Guelder rose	Deciduous. Beautiful autumn berries welcomed by wildlife. Medium, about 12 inches a year.
Hawthorn	Deciduous. The best windbreak. Quite fast. About 20 inches a year, perhaps more once it is established.
Holly	Evergreen. Can be quite formal. Slow, about 4 or 5 inches a year.
Holm oak	Evergreen. Can be quite formal. Reasonable, about 10 inches a year.
Hornbeam	Deciduous, though retains many of its leaves through winter. Quite fast, as much as 20 inches a year if things are going well.
Cherry laurel and Portuguese laurel	Evergreen. Very tough and suitable for shade. Fast, about 30 inches a year.
Bay laurel (as in the herb)	Evergreen. Requires sun and sharp drainage. Slow, about 5 inches a year, perhaps a bit more when it gets going.
Leylandii	Evergreen. Tough as old boots so long as you don't cut into it too deeply. Very fast, about 40 inches a year.

Privet	Essentially evergreen. Very beautiful flowers and useful berries. Can be kept as a formal hedge. Fast, as much as 20 inches a year in the right conditions.
Wild honeysuckle	Evergreen. Shaggy though formal with effort. Medium to fast, as much as 15 inches a year once it gets going.
Willow	Deciduous. Wispy and wants a damp soil. Very fast, 40 inches or more a year in the right conditions.
Yew	Evergreen. Wants sharp drainage. Slow to medium, if the leader has not been cut on planting may grow as much as 10 inches a year, very dependent on conditions into which it is planted.

– Pruning guide –

Pruning is mostly about bringing your garden to heel and cutting things back when they grow into places where you don't want them. However, it is also useful for removing dead, diseased or crossing wood and for encouraging a higher yield of fruit, flower or berry.

If coppicing is establishing a cutting point at or near ground level to encourage bushy multi-stemmed growth low down, pruning has the same effect higher up. Pruning is essentially aerial coppicing. But it is as well to remember that in most instances, when you prune a plant you are inviting it to create vigorous multi-stemmed growth. This is fine if it creates that growth into the space you intend, but certainly worth considering before you make the cut.

Actually the same logic applies even when you are cutting the grass. The more grass is cut the more healthy, vigorous and dense will its sward become. Regular cutting is the single best way to keep weeds and moss out of grass, if this is important to you.

Whilst all pruning involves establishing a cutting point, not all plants allow you to push them irretrievably back into a frame. As has been mentioned, some plants, like lavender and leylandii, won't break from dead wood, but most will.

The area below your cutting point can suffer from 'bare legs' syndrome. For example if you have an old rose with very bare legs at the back of a border you might choose to coppice a shrub in front of it to encourage new multi-stemmed growth and give it back its modesty. Alternatively, you could lower the cutting point on the rose to create bushy growth lower down.

By removing part of a plant (pruning) the parts which remain will benefit more from whatever its root system can deliver, and this is why pruning can be a useful aid to cropping. For example if you remove half the fruit on an apple tree at the beginning of July, the fruit that remains will grow bigger than it otherwise would have. Not only will each apple get more sun but it will be able to call on a larger share of whatever reserves the tree has to offer. If you want prize-winning dahlia flowers remove all but two or three of the fattest buds; if you want a few big roses prune away the spindly parts and so on.

Often the thing that confuses people most is not so much how to prune as when to:

Deciduous hedges	These are most often cut through the winter when other gardening jobs are less pressing. However, if you want hawthorn to put on a good display of blossom the following year cut no later than the beginning of July.
Evergreen hedges	A June cut and a further end of summer tidy if you want sharp lines through the winter. Evergreens ideally want to be cut after the last frost and well before the first one.
Roses	Climbing roses and those prone to wind rock in October, the rest by the end of February (perhaps by the end of March in the north).
Lavender	I prune mine in early spring when growth has just started, but if you want to keep them tight a second cut at the end of summer is necessary.
Clematis	Group one immediately after flowering, group two can be given a light prune after flowering, with a sterner one the following February, and those in group three are pruned in February.

Honeysuckle	Late flowering types pruned in the spring, early flowering types can be pruned immediately after flowering.
Apple and pear trees	A good midwinter job, when they are dormant.
Plum, cherry, apricot and peach	If pruned at all in early summer to avoid disease. Keep pruning minimal.
Deciduous flowering shrubs	For those that flower from July onwards (like buddleia) prune in early spring. For those that flower before July (like flowering currants) prune immediately after flowering.
Evergreen flowering shrubs	Sometimes immediately after flowering (such as with a daphne, though I wouldn't prune them at all myself) or in the case of something that flowers early, like Mahonia, delay pruning until as late as May. On balance I try not to prune evergreen flowering shrubs much anyway.

The following observations are generally well known but I repeat them just in case:

- Prune just above a bud on a plant, or as close to the join as possible with a tree.
- Make sure your blades are sharp and never press an undersized tool into an oversized job.
- If you're cutting a larger branch from a tree, run it down to the join in pieces rather than attempting a single cut and risking a tear.
- Don't bother painting cuts with wound dressing.

– Concluding Part V –

I hope in this section you have begun to see gardening in its wider context as essentially some sort of a partnership with trees, or at least as a tussle between trees and grasses. Just as the aurochs of old held woodland in check as they grazed, so we are the marauding herbivores of the twenty-first century, and this, I would suggest, gives us a certain amount of responsibility.

However, if we are to play the role of aurochs into the twenty-second century, we must look to our environment and start to take note. Plastic problems are embarrassing but if we lose pollinators the trouble will become a lot more immediate as tummies around the world begin to rumble. In a round-about way I hope this chapter has demonstrated two things: firstly, one of the most valuable things you can do for the environment remains to plant a tree or a hedge and secondly, as you start to see gardening in the wider context of landscape management, which means woodland management really, you will also start to spot ways in which you can use nature's essential direction of travel to your own advantage.

I hope this chapter has also given you a starting point for the answer to the question 'what tree?' or 'what hedge?' Certainly, you now know how to get them into the ground and what to do with them once they are in. Whilst we fulfil our role as modern aurochs, lopping a branch here or tidying a patch there, the boundless movement towards towering woodland is out there already. The wheel is spinning, the clay is turning in a great messy growing heap and if we manage to shape it just a little before it flies off the wheel we are fortunate.

Part VI

Bulbs & pots

– Clever little bulb –

If gardening is woodland management, the bulb reminds us that many plants have established cunning ways to survive in the shadow of their arboreal overlords. Spring flowering bulbs evolved to do their photosynthesising on the forest floor prior to leaf break. That is the only chance a bulb has under a closed canopy of deciduous woodland. Clever little bulb.

A bulb is an energy storage unit that enables the plant to throw up a shoot sufficient to reach the surface and photosynthesise. The goodness from this photosynthesis works its way back down into the bulb where it is stored for the following year when the same process happens again. This is why it is always hazardous to cut the foliage from any bulb after it has flowered because you are cutting off the supply of goodness it needs for flowering the following year.

To take a practical example, if you mow over a clump of daffodils immediately after they have flowered the chances are you will have a great number come up blind the following year, i.e. without flowers. If you repeatedly mow the foliage from the clump the daffodils will eventually expire and I have eradicated a few clumps using this method! It is a good idea to leave daffodil foliage for as long as possible before mowing and certainly until it starts to yellow. In borders, if the foliage is flopping all over the place and annoying you, it can be loosely tied up with some garden string and set to one side.

On planting, a bulb will have all the goodness it needs for that season already locked within it, so enriching soil prior to planting bulbs is largely pointless. However, after flowering the plant will start restocking for the following year so giving bulbs, particularly tulips, a quick liquid feed after flowering is a good idea.

All bulbs have a basal plate which is the fuzzy bit at the bottom from which the roots will grow. Basal plates can be delicate and so whether you are planting an onion, daffodil or tulip bear this in mind too. Similarly all bulbs have a growing point from which the stem will appear. As a general rule all bulbs should be planted at a depth equal to three times their height but as a general rule most bulbs also benefit from being planted just a smidgen more deeply than feels comfortable.

Oftentimes people make a fatal mistake when planting bulbs. It is understandable for a hominid with a logical mind to proceed to plant bulbs in an organised way, with equally spaced gaps or worse in straight lines. But if the hominid in question also wishes these bulbs to look natural when they have grown, he or she will be most disappointed. Nature doesn't plant daffodils in ugly straight lines, or with equal spacing, nature plants daffodils in unpredictable clumps. The best course is to cast out a handful of bulbs and plant them where they fall. Most of my efforts to eradicate daffodils have in fact been an attempt to cut holes in organised and not overly attractive lines of them!

Dahlias grow from tubers, crocuses from corms and bearded irises from rhizomes but they all represent soil based energy storage vessels, with the top growth used to restock the vessel for next year's show.

– What to plant –

Snowdrops & bluebells

There are a great number of snowdrop varieties and galan-thophiles get terribly carried away by the whole thing, sometimes paying hundreds of pounds for a single bulb. For me the joy of snowdrops, as the joy of bluebells, is to see thousands and millions of them rushing off into the distance, covering every fold and thicket of the scene before you. That said, snowdrops like life running along the side of a hedge and if you don't have space for a snowdrop wood (and I don't) then this is a perfectly good compromise. I also have a bed dedicated to snowdrops under a very large pear tree.

There are two systems for planting snowdrops. Either you can plant the bulbs in the autumn or you can wait and plant them 'in the green' in the spring. Some people say that they often fail if planted in the autumn but I have found if you buy good quality bulbs (which means ones that haven't dried out) they take perfectly well. Of course, the obvious advantage of planting them 'in the green' is that you can see where gaps in your snowdrop display are and plug them!

The picture for bluebells is much the same in terms of when and how to plant. Bluebells can be a good solution for a shady spot in the garden. It is important you buy our native bluebell (*Hyacinthoides non-scripta*) because the Spanish ones are invasive and have started crossing with ours. For this reason if you have Spanish ones you should really remove them. Our English fellows are in any case more delicate with attractive flowers falling to one side rather than thrusting matadorial spikes.

Winter irises

I love winter irises for their exotic little splash of colour early in the season. I grow them in flowerbeds and in pots, but it is the little pots of them in the spring that raise the largest smile. Winter irises flower nice and early in February and they grow from bulbs (unlike summer irises, the big ones, which grow from rhizomes).

Little pots can be brought into the house if you wish. I have a couple of favourites (Katharine Hodgkin is good and reminds me of the pale blue of the RAF uniform) but there is not much in it so choose whatever appeals to you. They should be planted just like snowdrop bulbs, the autumn before you want them.

Cyclamen

Cyclamen coum have a delicate sweptback-ness to their flower which is very appealing, and they can cope well with shade. I know this because when I first got here I planted a very showy variety I had bought on a whim. I forgot about it and it swiftly got overshadowed by a shrub. The other day I pushed some of the foliage from the shrub aside and found the little clump flowering happily away.

At Christmas, nurseries stock showy tender cyclamen and people tend to give them as gifts. These varieties will not survive in the garden. I think of little patches of cyclamen at

218

the foot of a large tree and it's a happy thought. Plant hardy cyclamen coum in the autumn.

Hyacinth

The Marmite of the gardening world, some people love the scent; others find it makes them feel sick. I think a whiff of hyacinth on an otherwise dreary January day brings a pleasure all of its own. If you want to enjoy hyacinths through the Christmas period you will need to start thinking about them in September. The best way is to buy prepared bulbs, which will take about six or seven weeks to flower. Pot them up, water them and place them in an unheated dark area (a shed outdoors). Check them periodically and when they are showing a couple of inches of growth bring them inside, give them a water and place them on a windowsill. If you pot a few up once a week you should have a decent supply through the darker months and they make good gifts too.

Any hyacinths I am given get stuffed in the garden when they are over and they always come up the following year. I have a special patch for them which expands by a few feet each winter.

Daffodils

If you want a great bank of daffodils to establish in grass it is worth choosing a variety that is known to naturalise; in other words one that has what it takes to 'go native'. Whilst some varieties of daffodil will do this readily others are more suited to the flowerbed. Our native daffodil, *Narcissus pseudonarcissus*, is unsurprisingly a good candidate for naturalising.

Believe it or not there are thirteen different classes of daffodil. There is no need to get acquainted with these classifications

219

unless you wish to become a daffodil expert (and I can think of worse things to be) but really for practical purposes other than the fact that some naturalise well and others don't there are two remaining important distinctions: colour and scent.

Some daffodils are yellow and some are white, often the white ones have an orange or red spot in the middle – in which case they are generally Pheasant's Eye – or they have a very delicate form with swept back ears like the terribly beautiful Thalia. The second distinction is that some smell strongly and others don't. I have found yellow daffodils tend to smell better than white ones and there is always room in my garden for what I consider the classic daffodil – a thumping great yellow with a large trumpet and strong smell.

A vase of daffodils seems to lift the smelt knowledge of spring and distribute it around a room. The more large vases per room the better. Some people go around dead heading daffodils so the plants don't waste energy creating seed. My children like being given this job and I am happy to swerve it.

You can use a bulb planter if you wish but I have found they often break. I use a spade to lift a square of turf the size of a paving slab and cast the bulbs into it. Excavate little holes under each bulb and then close the lid. Daffodils are best planted in September.

Muscari

Even through the bleakest parts of winter the little green stems of evergreen muscari keep photosynthesising away, so I can look out of my study window and see them and remember that the world will, in a few short months, be different again. It is something to hang onto. What they lack in size they make up for in delicate beauty.

Muscari, also called grape hyacinth, is a plant to carpet shady areas but also something to grow through gravel, in large clumps where it can break up proceedings very pleasingly. Various forms are available but they either flower blue or white and they either have large or small flowering spikes.

A few years ago I started a clump of quite large white ones (maybe Siberian Tiger) in a shady corner of a border and whilst this variety isn't evergreen (they emerge more like little green spiky stars in late winter) they have grown into a lovely colony that adds real uumph in March and April, just when it is needed. The time to move or subdivide a clump of muscari is in the summer when it is dormant, not in the spring when it is growing! I wouldn't be without my muscari and it is a strong candidate for a spring posy in an eggcup on my desk. Plant in the autumn for flowering the next year.

Crocuses

A pot of crocuses if a very fine thing but they reach the zenith of their crocus like life if planted in great swathes in sward. In fact, this is a bulb you *can* lay out in a geometric pattern, such as a large square in the middle of a lawn, or a circle around a showy tree. Crocuses come in yellow, white, blue and a sort of pink. For what it is worth, I am particularly fond of the striped purple and white Pickwick. Spring flowering crocuses are best planted in autumn for flowering the following year.

As an aside, it is perfectly possible to grow the saffron crocus (*Crocus sativus*) and in fact Saffron Walden in Essex is so named because a great deal of saffron was grown around it. For a decent crop you need a free draining soil in a sunny position and a lot of patience as you work round the flowers picking each stamen with a pair of tweezers. Saffron has a greater value by weight than gold.

The snake's head fritillary (*Fritillaria meleagris*) is quite different from the crown imperial (*Fritillaria imperialis*). The snake's head is a small bulbous perennial recognisable for its harlequin pattern of chequers, either shades of purple or white. It is hard to believe such an exotic looking thing is native to England, but it is. Despite the wholesale loss of meadowland in this country since the war – and whilst the sight of snake's head fritillaries would once have been common in the east and is now extremely rare – there are a few meadows in Suffolk that still have native wild growing populations.

Snake's head fritillaries are happiest in a damp patch of meadow but will survive well enough in most places, and sometimes look good in a circle around the base of a showy tree. I keep a few in pots outside my study to provide treasure for the eggcup on my desk. But if you want them to establish properly in grass, damp soil is essential. Bulbs are best planted in September.

The crown imperial fritillary is not native to England, coming originally from some exotic corner of Iran or Turkey, and will flower in early summer and provide a sunny patch of border with the floral equivalent of bling. Reaching to a height of three feet or more it provides a display that verges on being quite ridiculous, but which, I think, stays on just the right side of the line. They famously smell a little fetid, but this shouldn't put anyone off.

Gladioli

Gladioli have acquired an awful name, in part due to the fact that they have been most famously wielded by Dame

Edna Everage and therefore speak to her very funny rendition of the intolerably assured suburban housewife of 1950s Australia. But, gladioli are a very useful plant and deserve a comeback. They reach a good height and tolerate most soils. They come in all the colours of the rainbow and should be planted successively (every few weeks from March to May) for a continuous display, though I have patches that I have planted and half forgotten about and they come back each year.

Tulips

From Elizabethan times, tulips were greatly prized and collected by well-to-do gardeners around Europe who wished to show off. The Dutch became the master growers and there was a tulip boom in the seventeenth century (when investing in them got completely out of hand) which led to an inevitable tulip bust, since when tulip growing has been spared the attention of speculators.

Tulips must not be planted before November in order to avoid tulip disease, so don't just put them out with daffodils and snowdrops. If you ever get tulip disease you will want to rest the soil where they grew, and maybe even the garden as a whole, for a good number of years. There are a number of diseases that affect tulips and those that appear variegated with streaks of colour are in fact variegated on account of a tulip virus, but not one you have to worry about.

Traditionally people lifted their tulips after flowering and stored the bulbs in a dark shady frost-free corner of a shed until the following season. This is still a perfectly sensible way to make space for a follow-on crop of flowers, and many tulips will falter and fizzle if left in the ground, but I am interested in those that don't and over time have been testing varieties for their ability to return year in year out in the conditions I can give them.

Increasingly people who sell tulips will give you a steer on their survivability. If you have anything other than very free draining soil you will increase the chance of their healthy return by planting them onto a few inches of horticultural grit. The other thing to note is that some tulips grow very high, even to the point of needing support, and I find that if you plant the bulbs a little deeper than feels comfortable the stems enjoy a superior anchor and even quite tall tulips are less likely to flop.

Whilst most garden tulips are descended from ancestors who populated the Turkish mountains (which is why they like sharp drainage) there is in fact a wild native tulip in Britain which has a yellow flower and fine scent; however, like its more exotic cousins, it too wants sharp drainage. This would be a good candidate for establishing in grass with the right soil conditions but, whilst I haven't tried yet, I doubt it would prosper in our heavy soil.

Freesia

If you want freesias you can grow them in pots or in flower-beds, and if you have a cutting patch they are a must because they make especially fine cut flowers. Best to buy the corms and sow them successionally through the warmer months (from about April) to ensure a continuity of supply.

Freesias are not cold tolerant but neither are they expensive so you can lift them or just treat them as annuals.

Summer flowering irises

Summer flowering or bearded irises (so called because there are small hairs inside the flower) are princes of the garden and provide an exciting and exotic display in early summer. However, the downside is that after flowering they remain visually interesting only on account of their extraordinary lobster like rhizomes and spiky foliage. For this reason people often plant them either singly or in small clumps in amongst other flowers that will carry the show beyond June. There is a danger in this because the rhizomes themselves, which should be planted proud of the soil, love full sun and don't like to be shaded by neighbouring foliage. In fact, unlike the other plants covered in this section, best practice is to cut summer iris foliage back after flowering to within a foot of the ground, in order that the rhizome can really bake in whatever sun is available. I have a corner devoted to irises and when the flowers are gone enjoy ogling the rhizomes.

When planting irises, position the rhizomes themselves so they point south, or, given the circumstances, to the point that will receive maximum sun as this will ensure they get the greatest possible exposure to it. Irises should be planted on a bed of grit if you garden on a heavy soil. Whilst making space for irises requires a little thought, it is worth it.

There are in fact several different groups of irises and it is generally the case that the shorter ones flower earlier and the taller ones later. Rather than worrying too much about the technicalities the easy way to think about it is that there are irises which will grow to a few inches and spangle in late winter and then there are great thuggish irises that will billow in May and June – unless you intend to become an expert, leave it at that.

Dahlias

The thing that sets dahlias apart is the unique contribution they make to the garden in September, though all dahlias will be cut down by the first frost. Traditionally people would lift their dahlias at this point and store them in a cool dark place that never reaches below zero degrees (like an unheated cellar) and this is probably still best practice if you want to grow the very best flowers. Also, if you want to grow particularly large flowers, when the buds appear rub off all but two or three of the best.

The different varieties of dahlia are broken down into groups, as with daffodils, on account of the shape of their flower and there are at least nine or ten groups. I love all dahlias (literally, all of them): pom-pom, waterlily, cactus, the lot. I defy anyone not to be immediately thunderstruck with admiration; it would take a very cold heart indeed! However, as I have grown older I have given more and more of my heart over to the slightly less showy, and slightly subtler single-flowered varieties. I love the Bishop series for their darker foliage and floral simplicity.

Crocosmia

Also known as montbretia, for some not entirely discernible reason this was not a plant I bonded with particularly when I first met it. However, it has been growing on me lately for its delicate and enchanting flower. I have found a variety I like called Spitfire. It can be used to fill empty patches towards the front of a border. It is certainly an easy plant to multiply; every few years dig the clump up in spring, split it out and replant the segments. Shop bought bulbs can be planted in the spring also. It can take a year or two before they find their feet and start to flower strongly.

Colchicum

Little clumps of colchicum (pronounced Kol-Ki-Cum, at least by me anyway) look nice dotted along a border or around the base of a tree, particularly as they come out when everything else is going to sleep. They look quite like crocuses but actually are an entirely different family. Every part of the plant is extremely poisonous so be careful.

– *The power of a carefully positioned pot* –

Speaking personally I love an over-furnished room and I rail against minimalism excepting in very specific architectural circumstances. I don't quite know what maximalism means but I am for it! For a space to be human and comfy it usually needs more not less. I find the same aesthetic suits me in a garden and there is always room for another tub, pot, bucket or even wellington boot. The colour and texture of terracotta screams comfort, civility and warmth. A terracotta pot is one of the most immediate and gorgeous ways to banish austerity in a garden setting. That said, a pot on its own can look miserable; they are like sheep and suffer from a lack of company. Actually pots follow the same numeric rules as plants: groups of three, five, seven and nine are best. Exceptions are of course large single specimens (using a table for a frame, or a wellhead in the centre of a courtyard) or those that are an appendage to another structure, such as pots running along a wall.

As already mentioned, one distinct advantage to using pots is that you can carefully control the soil that you plant into (for rhododendron, azaleas etc). But another advantage is that you can control their position through the seasons, for example bringing tender plants in for the winter, moving something out into more sun or bringing it back for shade. Pots can add vertical interest and also make space for plants that like to tumble such as petunias, gypsophila or even ivy. Neither do pots have to be fiddly. I have a very simple low maintenance arrangement: a mat of creeping thyme under-planted with tulips. They can increase the growing area in a small garden (as with a vertical strawberry planter with grow-ing pockets all the way up its length), or provide opportuni-ties to grow plants in a space with no soil, like a terrace. It would be easy to dismiss pots as just one extra thing, but it would be a mistake.

– *What pot to use* –

This is ultimately a personal choice so fundamentally choose the one that pleases you best. However, there are some practical considerations. As mentioned, terracotta is undoubtedly a beautiful material; in fact, it is almost more than simply a beautiful material. It is somehow deeply human. It feels nice, it looks nice, it even smells nice. It is earthy and true and warm and lovely. It is, however, also porous and therefore behaves a bit like a wick below a paraffin lamp and unlike plastic will suck moisture out of the soil it contains. It is also expensive, heavy (particularly when filled with soil) and can crack in a sharp frost. All pots are heavy when filled with soil and larger ones should be moved with help and a special trolley.

Plastic, whilst having no inherent aesthetic appeal at all – and many other very grave disadvantages already discussed – is both light and retains the moisture within the soil it contains. As a result planting into plastic will mean watering less. If you want the benefits of plastic but the look of terracotta you can of course buy plastic pots to slip inside terracotta ones. This also makes transitioning from one pot display to another relatively easy (in go the new ones, out come the old ones).

There are other lightweight materials that are not plastic but are impervious to water. The RHS has a good line that they recently brought out, though they are not cheap. This is broadly speaking the direction of travel as far as I am concerned but it will take time and funds and I am not going to waste the pots I already have. If I had a gardener to water for me and if I lived in a different climate I would simply stick to terracotta.

All terracotta pots are 'earthenware' but not all earthenware pots are terracotta. Terracotta refers to the type of clay used and therefore the colour of the end product. If you are planning to use earthenware pots some brands mark their product as 'frost resistant' and generally these are the ones to go for. By raising your earthenware pot off the ground, either with purpose made little feet or, frankly, as I do, with bricks, you greatly reduce the risk of frost damage because heat rises and cold sinks and the ground in midwinter essentially becomes a convector for frost.

You can use any container you wish to hold soil and grow plants provided it has drainage holes at the bottom. It is surprising how often receptacles that might look promising, might even be being marketed for the purpose, don't have drainage holes! If the container in question is plastic, drainage holes can usually be made. I use a nail and a mallet and where possible I push the nail out from inside the pot (not the other way round, which would be easier) because I want the little torn flap of plastic to run with the water as it exits the pot not block the hole I have just created. Ultimately, whether it is an Italian terracotta pot or a pair of old wellies, or even a dustbin, so long as it has drainage holes it's a green light.

– To crock or not –

There is one final but critical matter which if you ignore could very well be your undoing. In the old days when an earthenware pot broke (not an uncommon experience) gardeners would keep all the shards in a drawer and they were called crocks. These crocks would be placed in the bottom of any new tub or container before adding compost to ensure the drainage holes in the bottom of the new tub or container didn't become silted.

Any drainage hole in the bottom of a pot has a very high chance of becoming clogged over time unless you use crocks. If the hole does become clogged the pot will become a swamp and the plants will die. On the other side of the equation, there is a downside to using sharp pieces of broken terracotta that become invisibly covered with soil. When it comes to planting back into that soil the chance of a nasty cut is high. But on the other hand, silting is life or death for the plants concerned. My solution is to use broken up pieces of polystyrene, the type used to protect delicate electronic equipment.

Debate rages about whether it is best to use crocks or not and some people allegedly don't though I don't know how they get by. I keep all polystyrene that comes to the house and break it up and place it in a dedicated storage bin in the barn. I try to use corner pieces for placing directly over drainage holes then I place flat pieces above them, then I position the odd larger stone to keep the whole in place, sprinkle over some horticultural grit and then add the compost! I personally believe this arrangement keeps the drainage holes open more or less indefinitely and I also believe it reduces the chance of nasty cuts to the radial artery. It also potentially reduces the chances of a pot cracking in the frost because the water, the part that will freeze and expand, drains out.

There is one final consideration. Even if you have done everything above to the letter to expertly preserve your drainage holes on the pot side, if you then plonk your pot onto bare soil there is every chance this will end up blocking the hole from the other side. All pots do better on a hard, uneven surface of brick, slate, cobble, paving slab or stone. As mentioned, you can buy little terracotta pot legs, though I don't tend to bother with these because they are a fiddle. When placing a pot on grass I arrange a few bricks under it first. So far I have never lost a pot – with the exception of one that was blown over by the wind and cracked. I fixed it with clear mastic.

– *Concluding Part VI* –

The idea that any of us could amble out on a Sunday afternoon and plant a handful of snowdrop bulbs and a century later there might be a never-ending carpet of them is beguiling. Snowdrops are reckoned to expand at the rate of an inch in circumference a year; but as the circumference itself expands so does the inch, exponentially. In other words an inch around a small clump in year three is quite different from an inch around a hundred clumps in year fifty. Bulbs will spread themselves around by seed too and this is why if you plant several different types of snowdrop you will, inevitably, end up with varieties that are all your own. One might even be favoured by galanthophiles and make you (or your grandchildren) lots of money!

This slow and steady accumulation of investments, the gradual enrichment of the landscape, is what gardening is all about; and gardeners are almost by definition people who are patient investors. That said, it is always possible to achieve a more immediate impact if you are prepared to put in the time and shoulder the cost. Having read this chapter I hope you will see the wider potential of the world of bulbs, beyond just snowdrops and daffodils.

The major drawback of pots is that you have to remember to water them more than you would plants growing in the ground, but think of the advantages. First, they are ultimately mobile. Friends who are renting houses often ask what they should do in the garden and I always say concentrate on pots. Pots are a legitimate place to grow bulbs, flowers, vegetables and even trees. It would be perfectly possible to have an amazing garden comprised of nothing but pots, and the skill in managing them is just the same.

Finally, just because you are using pots doesn't mean you shouldn't think about climbers and food. We have discussed how effective pots can be for growing herbs, particularly the Mediterranean ones which tolerate a somewhat arid soil, but any vegetable that can be grown in the ground can with care be grown in a pot. On a heavy soil several might even prefer life in a pot.

Part VII

Building projects & kit

– Hard landscaping –

Hard landscaping is expensive in time and money, and subject to the plea already made in this book to use plants where possible, hard landscaping undoubtedly does have the power to transform a garden; sometimes distinctly for the worse and at other times distinctly for the better. As has been mentioned it is critical to think about the ratios of green and grey, of natural and controlled, of dominated and released. Too much of one and you get a wildlife garden (no bad thing), too much of the other and you get a brownfield site. Also the wages of a wrong decision are high. Tearing up a recently constructed path, terrace or wall is so painful as to be done only by the most committed gardener, and a mistake can therefore inch into the longer term.

Once you have carefully considered your scheme the question becomes whether you should call in an expert or attempt to do it yourself. By now you know I am a 'have a go' sort of gardener. I have attempted quite a lot of building jobs myself with various degrees of success but I have never yet regretted trying.

There are certain jobs within building that are highly specialised and require both knowledge and skill to be undertaken safely. Within this category I would include any electrical work, but also roofing, thatching and anything beyond basic plumbing. Even a wall to three feet needs a proper footing and any wall will clearly present a health and safety issue if it falls over! Still, there is no magic to any building job. The difference between you and me on the one hand and a master craftsman on the other is the speed with which we can work and the quality of the final product. But speed and quality might not be the ultimate driving factors; very often serviceability is good enough.

– *Where to buy the basics* –

The first thing to say is that in a newly acquired garden there may be at least some stuff lying around. Whilst I admit my garden is larger than average, I found two oak sleepers hiding in the bottom of a hedge which I dredged out and both became benches. An old raised bed got moved into a more favourable position and I found a good quantity of paving stones under a shed which have gone into making several paths. It pays to have a thorough rootle around. Existing features which you don't like usually present a wealth of raw materials which, with a little thought, might present the opportunity for upcycling into a feature that you do like.

Thankfully in this country we are blessed with a good number of builders yards and hardware shops so it is important to find out where your nearest ones are. A good builders yard should stock not just essential tools (from mastic guns to wire cutters) but a fair range of timber, stone and brick, not to mention bags of cement, sand and gravel. After a knife, ball of string and secateurs, iron fencing pins are the most useful item in my garden; I use them for supporting young trees, making temporary wigwams, securing barn doors and as dibbers – over time they rust down pleasantly too.

Finally, some building materials can be bought at the larger

241

plant nurseries themselves. In addition to tubs, pots and edging boards many nurseries will stock stepping stones, gravel and things like landscape fabric or pond liner. The internet is useful when only one type of string will do.

– *Digging a pond* –

Ihave previously said that the single most important thing
you can do for insects is to plant a tree. This is probably
only true if you already have a pond. Insects need to drink,
and bees will sip from the surface of the pond, using a lily pad
as a landing strip. Would you like to see a bee at the watering
hole? Birds need a drink and so do mammals. Ponds therefore
act as a giant magnet to local wildlife, which makes them
irreplaceably important viewing platforms for those of us
who like nature.

Many people seem to think that digging a pond is a difficult project that is somehow beyond them, but a perfectly
good pond can be the job of a weekend or perhaps two. In
fact, there are good horticultural reasons for not making your
pond too deep. The deepest part of your pond need be no
more than two feet with a good run of shelf at about eight
inches. This is because whilst some aquatic plants, notably
water lilies, want to be planted a little deeper the bulk of
aquatic plants you might fancy growing (water mint, water
forget-me-not, water iris) are best planted on a shelf at about
eight inches.

The final structural consideration is that you want an area
of beach, i.e. a gently sloping ramp into and out of the pond.
This helps creatures who want to come and drink but also
mammals who might fall in and then feel the need to get out

again. If you are making a larger pond a beach is an important safety feature for humans too!

When you choose a site for your pond think of it as what it is: an aquatic flowerbed. Just like a normal flowerbed it will want a good amount of sun, so don't site it under a run of large trees, not least because in addition to blocking the sun their litter will be an annoyance. Like a flowerbed, you want it to be somewhere where you can easily enjoy it, no point throwing your pearls among swine. Nice, perhaps, to be able to see it from the kitchen sink? Many aquatic plants, like the marsh marigold which is a particular favourite of mine, put on an awesome early flower display.

In this region farmers would dig a hole to gather clay for the construction of their house and then be left with a crater that could become a pond for keeping ducks and sometimes fish. Typically they would drive sheep through it to seal the bottom but unless you have both clay and sheep it is probably best to purchase some pond liner from your local nursery. Sometimes it pays to put an under liner below this, for example old carpet, as you don't want to acquire a leak if your pond liner isn't all that thick and your soil is full of sharp flints.

Once the pond has been dug there is always a question of what to do with the spoil. For a smallish sized pond it is often perfectly possible to use this to further articulate the edges of the pond itself and to lose the rest in the approach. Then comes the matter of fitting the lining. Standing on it can help to spread it nice and evenly into the various cracks and crevices and it is often useful to use large stones to weigh down parts as you go. These can ultimately become features lying just under or gently cresting the surface of the water.

Once the liner is in, the pond must be filled. Technically the best thing to do is to wait for it to be filled with (largely chemical free) rainwater but if you are anything like me I doubt you will have the patience for this. So alternatively fill it up with tap water, but leave it for a few days before planting into it to allow the chlorine to burn off.

If all this still seems too much like hard work it can be fun to construct a small pond, perhaps with little people, from no more than an old washing up bucket. Even a mini pond can be a remarkably useful resource for birds and insects.

– Four absolute essentials for any garden –

When I lived in London I ran my garden with four essential pieces of kit: hand secateurs, a hand trowel, a watering can and large quantities of string. Though I needed a spade to dig over the beds in the first place (I think I borrowed one) I generally used the secateurs to cut the string. As such, I would say these are the four essential pieces of kit for any garden, large or small.

Hand secateurs

There are two basic differences when it comes to hand secateurs. One type has an anvil that the blade is pushed down into, the other system has two blades which cross each other as you snip – like scissors. Of these two I find the latter a better system because with the former, for one reason or another, the blade stops falling perfectly onto the anvil and you end up tearing plant flesh as you cut.

I have also found that the quality of manufacture is crucial, with a pair using the blade and anvil system from a good brand potentially outperforming a pair using the crossing system from a not so good brand. Whatever type you use it is imperative to keep the blades sharp and having a quick go over them with a sharpening stone should become a habit. How the thing sits in your hand is the most important factor of all – it should feel comfortable for you, so hold and snip with several pairs before heading for the checkout.

It is remarkably easy to cut the end of a finger off with a sharp pair of secateurs and I have had some near misses. This sort of thing usually happens because you are rushing or thinking about something else. I don't let my children use secateurs unless I am standing over them and holding them too.

Hand trowel

I do prefer tools with wooden handles but this is not essential. In essence there are hand trowels with wide faces (known as spits) and others with narrow ones. The narrow-faced ones are far more useful because whilst they can be used for a bit of digging, anything they can't cope with I use a spade for anyway. In the meantime, however, being thin, they are far more useful for leveraging out weeds with a long taproot like thistles, without upsetting valuable neighbours.

I often use my trowel with a narrow spit and rarely if ever use one with a wide spit. Incidentally, I don't use a trowel as if it were a small spade with the face pointing away from me. Rather, when digging a planting hole or some such, I find holding the trowel with the face of the blade facing me and then stabbing downwards and pulling the soil back towards me the most ergonomic way to do it.

Watering can

There are two aspects to a watering can. The first is the amount of water that it can carry and the second is the size of the rose through which the water comes out. In gardening terms the amount of water it carries is secondary to the size of the rose because a small rose enables us to water seed trays and pots without washing the recently sown seed away, whereas a large rose enables the fast watering of a larger area. In an ideal world you will have both capacities though that might still only mean a single watering can if it comes with different sizes of rose.

Counterintuitively, the correct way to fix a rose onto a watering can is so the face of the rose, the part with the holes in it, is pointing up at the sky, not down at the ground. This means that when pouring the water drops fall evenly as rain rather than in a dripping line as with a broken shower. Of course, metal watering cans are very nice to look at but speaking personally I have watering cans of all sorts and sizes dotted around the place.

String

String is not just string. Cooking string (which I have often fallen back on when I have run out of garden string) is not nearly so good. First, it is bleached white so looks odd in the garden, second it is thin and sharp so cuts into plants and third it is weak. What you need is proper jute twine which has a softer edge so will do less damage to plant stems and yet is strong, and preferably of a shade that will melt into the background of the garden.

Remember Hilaire Belloc's Henry King whose chief defect was chewing little bits of string! It may sound obvious but don't try to bite through pieces of string: it is an open invitation to crack a tooth – you need a penknife or scissors to cut it.

– Kit for the larger garden –

When we moved to the house we live in now I suddenly needed all sorts of pieces of kit that I hadn't needed in London. It may sound odd, but I distinctly remember the sheer pleasure of thrusting with a lawn edger for the first time (and seeing a nice crisp edge appear as I went). But my requirements didn't stop at a lawn edger; I needed an axe, a new spade, forks, rakes and sharpening stones to say nothing of two new lawn mowers and much else besides. So here I share my thoughts on larger pieces of kit and machinery.

Axe

Axes were in fact the original human piece of 'kit' and can be dated to the Paleolithic period about 1.7 million years ago. This predates our emergence as *Homo sapiens* by well over a million years. *Homo sapiens* means 'wise man' but his ancestor, *Homo erectus* or 'upright man', was merrily wielding flint axes with results we can only guess at. There is a haunting scene in *2001: A Space Odyssey* when an ape picks up a bone and intentionally bangs it on the ground, suddenly realising it has potential as a tool. In the next scene he is braining another animal. Clever might have been a more accurate description for our species than wise; but in any case it is at least likely that the age of reason and the age of the axe were born together.

Axes were not just used for killing enemies or acquiring food but for digging too. We didn't move from axe to spade for a long time and perhaps that was because an axe, even today, can be quite useful when digging, particularly digging out roots.

The key to a good modern axe is weight and balance. Ideally you want the weight of the head of the axe falling to do the work for you. Most importantly you need to keep the blade of the axe sharp. Axes come with both metal and wooden handles and there are short handled and long handled versions. If you only have one axe, go for a traditional long handled one with a wooden shaft and then when you can add a short handled metal one do. If you haven't used an axe before get a lesson first.

I don't own a chainsaw and I would strongly caution against anyone using one until they have gone through proper training. If you have just bought a home in the country and you fancy playing around with a chainsaw, don't. If you are married to such a person, stop them. The thing about a chainsaw is they have a habit of driving up and off the object they are cutting. If this happens they may well drive up and off into the head of the person who is holding them. I know myself and I push myself too hard when tired; the wages of doing this with a chainsaw are simply too high. If using a chainsaw, proper protective clothing including a helmet and goggles must be worn at all times.

Generally the danger with an axe is that it glances off the object it is meant to be cutting and into the leg of the person wielding it, or if really unlucky, perhaps into the leg of someone standing next to him or her. Both accidents are to be avoided but a chainsaw in the head is probably worse than an axe in the leg. My father-in-law put an axe in his leg and it didn't stop him playing near professional level tennis; I am not sure that a chainsaw in the head would have left him so nifty on court.

Spade

If an axe represents ancient technology a spade is cutting edge! To break as well as move earth you really need metal, and spades didn't arrive properly until we started working with metal in earnest. Bronze Age spades have been found in Britain, but they don't look particularly effective. Roman spades look like they might have been better but I suspect the age of the spade only really took off with the mass production of steel. This means the spade as we know it has only been readily available for a hundred and fifty years.

A beautifully balanced spade with a wooden shaft and sharp spit creates a pleasure in the use that is all of its own. A wooden shafted spade is of course generally more expensive than its all metal equivalent (the latter can be bought for peanuts in most large supermarkets) but there is simply no joy in using a heavy metal spade. I have broken many a wooden shaft, usually with a fork, trying to lever out a heavy tree or shrub in a hurry. On the other hand, most local hardware shops will fix your shaft for you.

There are as many different types of spade as there are materials that people have wished to dig into but in all cases there is one important point to consider: the heavier the weight of the material to be excavated the smaller the spit of your spade should be. From a gardener's perspective, if you garden on heavy often waterlogged clay you may not wish to have a massive spit on your spade because each spadeful will be heavier. On the other hand if you are on a sandy, light and free draining soil you could 'afford' a larger spit. In either case a shovel is entirely different from a spade. If you could only have one it would have to be a spade. A spade can also be used to shovel; whereas a shovel can never be used in place of a spade. A spade is for cutting into a material, a shovel is only ever for moving it.

Knife

Preference for a pocket knife is a highly personal thing. Whichever knife you go for it must be comfortable in your pocket and the blade kept sharp. I would question the suit-ability of a knife that doesn't slip easily into and out of the pocket but that would be my only criterion, and some people keep them attached to a belt with a holster.

I have a thin and light stainless-steel knife with a single fold-ing blade to about five inches. The end of the blade has a slight hook which can be useful when removing a little branch, twig or stem but makes sharpening it a little less easy. It also ever so slightly increases the need for manual dexterity when cutting string. Since I most often use my knife for cutting string I have considered getting a new one with a similarly no nonsense handle but a shorter, straighter blade. I think a blade length of no more than two inches might be optimum.

Fork

Historically a wide range of forks were produced, each with a different use. In the modern world these seem to have been melted down into what seems to be a standard single size and shape which carries just a bit too much compromise to be useful for certain jobs.

A hay fork, unsurprisingly, was used for stacking hay and it has a wide open face with light narrow points. If you tried moving hay with a modern garden fork not only would it take you twice the time but you would get tired very quickly. Actually, I quite often have use for a hay fork, for example when moving leaves around the place or managing the bonfire. On the other hand a hay fork could never be used for breaking up soil. For this purpose the current standard form is acceptable.

Incidentally, you always want to dig over an already cultivated patch of soil with a fork, not a spade. Forks are useful for working goodness into the soil but they are absolutely essential for moving plants. When moving an established shrub you want to work around it with a fork, pushing the soil in towards its root ball as you go, before gently prising. Using a fork ensures as much of its root system is preserved as possible; a spade would merely slice the bulk of it off.

Gloves

I strongly dislike the sensation of wearing gloves in the same way that I prefer sleeveless jumpers and jackets so my shoulders aren't restricted. Besides I can be clumsy and when I weed wearing gloves I end up pulling all the flowers up. I have a pair of plastic gloves for particularly disgusting jobs like clearing out the wallop in the chicken coop or, worse, plunging our drains, and I have my father's old pair of yellow leather gardening gloves which I reluctantly use for work on Rugosa roses. I also use them when I am cutting back stretches of blackthorn. The spikes of blackthorn are not only fearsome, they are also poisonous, so an argument with one can lead to a trip to the doctor. Leather gloves can be useful when grabbing a creature that you don't want to bite or sting you too.

Wheelbarrows

There is nothing quite so frustrating as getting to the point in a job when you know you need the wheelbarrow, locating it and then finding that it has a flat tyre. Whilst this can often be dealt with by giving it a quick pump and resolving to fix the puncture properly at a later date, you never do and the sorry saga continues. As a result I am a strong convert to the new punctureless tyre system on wheelbarrows; I really do think it is worth it.

Quite often when collecting leaves, or the detritus from hedge cutting, a wheelbarrow just doesn't seem to hold enough material. In these circumstances there is an argument for a trolley with a long handle or a small trailer that can be pulled by a ride-on lawnmower. That said, both are a fiddle. It is also possible to buy special sides that you slot into your wheelbarrow to increase the volume of material it can transport. However, nine times out of ten I wait until the wheelbarrow is almost full and then I drive a couple of long wooden cuttings into it on either side which creates a sort of basket. As you fill up the space in between, keep adding the odd vertical stick from the waste you cut and it is perfectly possible to double the amount of material you can fit into a normal wheelbarrow without the expense of buying extras or the fiddle of hooking up trailers.

Rakes

It would be impossible to run this garden without rakes (plural). There are a very large number of rakes, each designed for a special task and sometimes useless at doing anything else. I have found the leaf rake and soil rake to be essential.

A leaf rake should have a wide light head and can have blunt tines. This is principally used for gathering leaves in the autumn and the mess you create when you cut a hedge. Remember the wider the head the quicker it is to clear a large area. Sharp metal tines can end up skewering lots of leaves and this can be annoying.

A soil rake wants a small-ish head more or less in the shape of a hammerhead shark. It can have thick-ish metal tines but they don't want to be too long. Unlike a leaf rake you don't want the biggest head you can find because a big head will be unwieldy, particularly if you are working inside or next to vegetables. Also a large head would be heavy and quite a lot of time is spent smashing this rake into soil to break it up. This is the rake you will use to create the 'fine tilth' beloved of textbooks when you are sowing seeds. This is the rake of the vegetable patch!

Ladders

A ladder is essential for all manner of different jobs from clearing gutters to cutting hedges. Japanese gardeners use three-legged tripod style ladders which are very stable and best for getting into tight spots. They are available in the UK but quite expensive. For many years I have used my conventional ladder, often set with its front legs deep within the architecture of the hedge as I climb it. I always check its stability quite robustly before making the ascent and of course for anything that is even vaguely perilous it is useful to have someone at the other end holding it. Some people use special trestles for hedge cutting, which is probably sensible.

It was years before I realised the truly transformational benefit of sharpening all cutting edges including things like axes
and spades. Would you think to sharpen the spit on your
spade? It was also years before I realised how complex and
yet crucial the whole area of sharpening is, particularly when
it comes to types of sharpening equipment. It was only very
recently that a friend pointed out to me that the best way to
keep a wood saw functional is to periodically bend the little
teeth out in alternate directions. If you look at an ordinary
builder's saw in a shop you will notice the little teeth are reso-
lutely pointed alternately outwards. If you look at an old saw
in your shed you will notice they are not. These teeth should
themselves be sharpened from time to time too, which of
course requires a sharpening file of suitable size.

In fact, by my estimation, sharpening blades usually reduces
the amount of effort required, whether digging, sawing, slash-
ing or chopping, by as much as half. This garden wouldn't
run without the good offices of a fleet of sharpening devices.
If you only have two you want a large one man enough to
address things like axes and spades. Mine is cigar-shaped
with a bulge in the middle, perhaps as long as my forearm,
and it looks a bit like a miniature Obelix of Asterix and
Obelix fame. But then you also need a sharpening file and
these can either look a bit like a chisel (with a blunt end) or
sometimes like a Roman dagger (with a spiky one). The ones
that look like a Roman dagger are best because they can be
used to get into the teeth of a hedge cutter but also, for example, to sharpen the small teeth of a saw.

I do not know why this is the case, but I have found that
you should only ever run the stone or file along the blade in
the same direction, never in both directions, if you wish to

achieve a really sharp edge quickly. The picture of the chef running his carving knife terrifyingly quickly up and down a kitchen knife sharpener is not instructive. Instead think of the steady hands of the carpenter, usually pushing the stone or file away from himself slowly. Stopping. Disconnecting. Then coming back to undertake the same action again.

Mowers

The most important decision you have to make before buying a ride-on lawnmower is what width of cutting deck you want. They vary but are typically between three and five feet in width. This decision can even play a part in how the structure of your garden evolves because from that day on it is tempting to size things to fit the mower you have. For example, it makes sense for a grass path to be the width of one or two sweeps with the mower but not really one and a half. It also makes sense to have gates that permit the mower through. It stands to reason that the wider the cutting deck the better if you have larger amounts of grass to get through, but a narrower deck will be required for negotiating more intimate spaces, so as with everything, there is a trade off.

The second decision to be made when you buy a ride-on mower is whether it should be one that collects grass or mulches it as you go. A mulch mower cuts each piece of grass several times and then spews it out as you go along. This has a number of effects. First, it means that the goodness from the cutting is being directly returned to the soil. This is good if you want to favour grasses but not so good if you are trying to gradually reduce the quality of the soil in order to favour wildflowers. Second, it means that it is not possible to achieve quite the same level of neatness (think orderly stripes in the grass) as if you pick up the cuttings. On the other hand if you collect grass you need to keep stopping to empty the collection chamber and you need somewhere to compost it all.

All ride-on mowers, whether a mulching or collection system is used, should have the ability to adjust the cutting deck from roughly an inch in height to roughly five, though the greater flexibility the better. I have a ride-on with a mulching system and a cutting deck to roughly five feet in width. I also have a small push mower with a collector for the places the ride-on just can't get into.

My push mower is relatively traditional in construction and what this means is it is quite heavy. It has a motor that drags it forward for me but its weight still makes turning and guiding boring. Mine has a petrol two-stroke engine and it is therefore noisy and generous with its fumes. I think if I had a smaller garden, or if I were starting over, I might look for an electric solution.

Hedge cutters and strimmers

These can be very expensive. Whether you are buying a hedge cutter, strimmer, mower or any other power machinery there has always been a concern in my mind that unscrupulous dealers will sell you underpowered kit safe in the knowledge that you will shortly be back for something with more guts. Getting something that is man enough and high quality enough for the task you have in mind first time round will always save you money overall.

When we first moved here, I bought a short handled posh hedge cutter with a petrol engine and I am delighted that I did. It has never failed me and it has always been able to do more than I asked it. The brand is known to be excellent and certainly I am a big fan. However, because I had spent so much on a top quality short handled hedge cutter I shied from buying a long handled hedge cutter at all. In fact, anxious to buy trees and plants, I put off buying a long handled hedge cutter for several years.

Eventually I could take it no longer and I went out to buy a long handled hedge cutter, but still generally of the opinion that I didn't want to explain a purchase of c. £800. As such I spent a quarter of that amount. Sadly I quickly discovered that it was heavy and, worse, would overheat and just cut out. Cutting hedges with it became an exercise in not getting angry.

None of this matters now because I have adjusted my whole approach to hedge cutting. I don't cut every hedge every year and those I do cut I allow myself the whole winter to go at rather than trying to do them all in ten days in the autumn. Not only have I permitted myself more time, I now principally use telescopic bypass loppers and a pruning saw to take out all thicker branches, then I use ultra light hedge shears to tidy up. I only occasionally spark up my old and trusty short handled hedge cutter. Hedge cutting now takes longer but it is far, far more enjoyable and there is very little noise, just me at the top of a hedge occasionally pausing to enjoy the view.

If you are to have a long handled hedge cutter consider investing in a harness. They look like rucksacks with wires coming off but they transfer the weight of the cutter to your hips and save your arms, torso, back and neck.

Strimmers are the only piece of garden equipment that I genuinely loathe. I dislike handling them, I dislike the noise they make and worse the more powerful ones use cutting string at the end that always tangles. They can also do serious damage to trees in the hands of the careless and if you aren't the one who wields them (and even if you are) it can pay to secure plastic tree guards to a foot in height around the base of young trees for this reason. The smaller electric ones, which tend to use easily replaceable plastic blades, are by comparison a dream to use, and they are good for giving the place a general tidy, but can't take on anything substantial.

– *Basic equipment for seed sowing* –

The standard basic size of pot most often referenced on seed packets is 3 inch or 7.5 cm (which describes its circumference at the top). It is large enough to hold most seedlings for a good while whilst not so large as to risk them damping off in soil that simply holds too much water. If you only had one size of pot it would be this one. If you added a size you would add a smaller pot for seedlings particularly prone to damping off.

I find a 3.5 inch pot useful for saplings that I know will be sitting in their pot just a little longer. I have come to the conclusion that square pots are generally speaking better than round ones because they encourage the roots into the corners from where they can break new ground when planted out rather than round and round in a corkscrew, which is a habit they may find hard to break.

It is now also possible to buy compostable pots made from cardboard or coir. These allow you to plant them straight into the ground when the plant reaches a certain size. This has the advantages of not having to disturb the roots, adding organic matter to the soil and it is environmentally friendly – however, I have found two drawbacks. The coir or cardboard can behave like a wick and draw moisture out from the soil around the plant's roots. The answer is to bury the sides of the pot under soil too. Also, the ones made from a cardboard type material can become mouldy though it doesn't seem to hurt the plants inside. This is clearly the direction of travel but I have so many old plastic pots it seems wasteful not to use them until they have no life left in them first.

There are two basic sizes of seed tray: full size which is about fifteen inches long and half that size which is about eight. I hardly ever use my full-sized seed trays now because so often the crops you need a seed tray to start are ones that you start successionally (like salad) throughout the season and therefore the rule is little and often. If I were starting again I would buy more half-size trays than large ones, perhaps three to one, but when I first got going in fact I did the opposite.

Cheaper seed trays constructed of thin pressed plastic will crack and tear over time. These cracks and tears can be remedied with strips of robust masking tape but better if possible to buy ones that have been made with a thicker plastic, the type that won't bend. Another advantage to these higher end seed trays is that the lids often have ventilation strips that can be opened or closed. If you do have lids with no ventilation strips the lids can be held up by resting on a plant label (matchstick style).

Sandwich bags should be over eight inches deep and it is helpful if they have the sticky self-sealing lines at the opening because these can be stuck around pots and will remain good enough for the job for a remarkably large number of seasons. When the stickiness eventually fades elastic bands can be used to secure them. These are a crucial part of my seed-sowing armoury and create excellent little greenhouses over newly sown seeds. On the other hand we all have a growing awareness of the importance of reducing our use of plastics, and we gardeners have historically been among the worst offenders. Despite being carefully stored each winter my sandwich bags are getting to the point where they will have to be retired. If weighed against the vast quantities of produce (peas, beans, courgettes, squashes, tomatoes etc) which have started out life under them over the last six years, and the amount of plastic packaging that would otherwise have been involved if all that produce had been brought back from the shops, I suspect the balancing equation is still in favour of the sandwich bags. All the same, I am searching for an alternative solution.

Plant labels come in plastic, wood or metal. What matters is that you have a pen that works with the material selected. I try to scratch old marker pen markings off my plastic ones and reuse them, or I simply use them for the same crop the next season. Once these are no longer useful I will increasingly rely on wood.

As with sandwich bags, an atomiser or mister is an indispensable part of my seed-sowing armoury. All seedlings and cuttings that have their foliage gently misted from time to time will do better than those that don't. Also, it is a useful way of providing initial water to very fine seeds that might otherwise be washed away. Periodically the nozzle clogs and the spray comes out in a restricted and irritating manner. I use a sewing needle to clear the nozzle when this happens. My atomiser has been with me since the start of my seed-sowing days! A very good way to economise on disinfectant spray and cut down the amount of plastic you use generally is to pick up an extra atomiser at the garden centre and then mix your own spray from the largest screw top bottles of disinfectant you can find.

– *Concluding Part VII* –

Ihope this section has given you the confidence to think about starting a project in your own garden. What is so nice about these sorts of jobs is that they can often be shared with friends who can be rewarded for their labours with a nice lunch drawn from the vegetable patch afterwards. A huge amount of fun can be had, and progress made, over the course of a single weekend and the sense of achievement when all is complete can set the tone for life generally and send you and your friends back to work on a Monday with a renewed spring in your step.

So often in life we have to work towards things (like paying down mortgages) that seem to be interminable, so a new pond, say, which has a defined beginning, middle and end can provide a relatively immediate sense of achievement. Sometimes, for all of us, life can feel a bit like trying to push spaghetti up a hill and at these times even a little project outdoors can be just what the doctor ordered.

Of course, even when a pond is finished it has only really just started, and that is true of all garden projects. In the case of a pond, dozens of different species will over time make it their home and there is a real pleasure in simply noting its progress. In fact this can carry the sense of achievement forward through weeks, months and years. This same logic applies even to a brick path. Over time the appearance of the path will melt gently into the garden as a whole and if you have provided little slips and cracks for planting creeping thyme these plants will grow and flower and spread their babies around finding little toeholds all of their own to join the lichens and moss that will inevitably develop. Everything in a garden, even the built parts, are dynamic and this is certainly more than half the joy.

Conclusion

My garden, Skymeadow, is a place of rest, a place to hide, an impossibly private place to be truly shared only with those I love most especially. But it is also in some mysterious sense a place of work, a place in which I can be found and a place that repays the investments I make in it with great dollops of crazy interest. Skymeadow started as an idea, it remains an idea. But it is emergent and real too. Gardens are places where the imagination can hover over the waters of reality; where the two can meet and play and dance under the clear light of a bright moon.

This morning I found a new little colony of field mice down by the elm hedge. Yesterday, I saw the avenue under a gentle autumn sun, the sort of golden light that casts unthreatening shadows. The day before I cut the orchid lawn and noticed the yews I planted six years ago had put on at least fifteen inches of growth over the summer. It has been a phenomenal year for butterflies, moths, damsel and dragonflies. I still can't believe it. This is a garden that just keeps giving.

Skymeadow is a companion to Sybilla and I as we navigate the vicissitudes of life. It has its own clock, it keeps its own time. The children have already started growing up within it just as the hedges we planted have. Each year it is both different and the same. Each season it is both familiar and new. This garden gives me something very precious, something akin to a gentle life affirming hum. I try to share that hum with other people, some of whom I know, others of whom I may never meet, but all of whom I hope will derive from it some of the benefit I do.

None of this would have been possible if I hadn't first put my fear down and picked my secateurs up. If I hadn't roughly ordered aside that little nagging voice that said, 'You don't know what you are doing'. From that one act of defiance much greater acts of defiance have followed. It might have been otherwise. This garden might have only ever been something someone else cut. Imagine that?

Let your garden be both friend and tutor. Let it build your self-confidence and remind you of what manner of creature you are. As we tear down the veil of fear that keeps us from our gardens, will we find a new way of looking at tangled knots in other parts of our lives? Remember the garden's lessons. Don't get weighed down by the past. Don't get weighed down by the future. Life can't be just a worrying list of jobs. No fear gardening, no fear life.